SAY NO TO NEGATIVES

J.P. Vaswani

BALBOA.
PRESS
A DIVISION OF HAY HOUSE

Balboa Press books may be ordered through booksellers or by contacting:

Balboa Press
A Division of Hay House
1663 Liberty Drive
Bloomington, IN 47403
www.balboapress.com
1-(877) 407-4847

Because of the dynamic nature of the Internet, any web addresses or
links contained in this book may have changed since publication and
may no longer be valid. The views expressed in this work are solely those
of the author and do not necessarily reflect the views of the publisher,
and the publisher hereby disclaims any responsibility for them.

The author of this book does not dispense medical advice or prescribe the use
of any technique as a form of treatment for physical, emotional, or medical
problems without the advice of a physician, either directly or indirectly. The
intent of the author is only to offer information of a general nature to help
you in your quest for emotional and spiritual well-being. In the event you use
any of the information in this book for yourself, which is your constitutional
right, the author and the publisher assume no responsibility for your actions.

Any people depicted in stock imagery provided by Thinkstock are models,
and such images are being used for illustrative purposes only.
Certain stock imagery © Thinkstock.

Printed in the United States of America.

ISBN: 978-1-4525-7887-3 (sc)
ISBN: 978-1-4525-7889-7 (hc)
ISBN: 978-1-4525-7888-0 (e)

Library of Congress Control Number: 2013913749

Balboa Press rev. date: 10/17/2013

Books and Booklets by J.P. Vaswani

7 Commandments of the Bhagavad Gita
10 Commandments of a Successful Marriage
108 Pearls of Practical Wisdom
108 Simple Prayers of a Simple Man
108 Thoughts on Success
114 Thoughts on Love
A Little Book of Life
A Little Book of Wisdom
A Simple and Easy Way To God
A Treasure of Quotes
Around The Camp Fire
Be An Achiever
Be in the Driver's Seat
Begin the Day with God
Burn Anger Before Anger Burns You
Comrades of God - Lives of Saints from East & West
Daily Appointment with God
Daily Inspiration (A Thought for Every Day of The Year)
Daily Inspiration
Destination Happiness
Dewdrops of Love
Does God Have Favorites?
Finding Peace of Mind
Formula for Prosperity
Friends Forever
Gateways to Heaven
God In Quest of Man
Good Parenting
How to Overcome Depression
I am a Sindhi
I Luv U, God!
India Awake
Joy Peace Pills
Kill Fear Before Fear Kills You
Ladder of Abhyasa
Lessons Life Has Taught Me
Life after Death

Life and Teachings of Sadhu Vaswani
Life and Teachings of the Sikh Gurus: Ten Companions of God
Living in the Now
Management Moment by Moment
Mantras for Peace of Mind
Mantra for the Modern Man
Many Paths: One Goal
Many Scriptures: One Wisdom
Nearer, My God, To Thee!
New Education Can Make the World New
Peace or Perish: There Is No Other Choice
Positive Power of Thanksgiving
Questions Answered
Saints For You and Me
Saints With A Difference
Secrets of Health And Happiness
Shake Hands With Life
Short Sketches of Saints Known & Unknown
Sketches of Saints Known & Unknown
Spirituality in Daily Life
Stop Complaining: Start Thanking!
Swallow Irritation Before Irritation Swallows You
Teachers are Sculptors
The Goal Of Life and How To Attain It
The Highway to Happiness
The Little Book of Freedom from Stress
The Little Book of Prayer
The Little Book of Service
The Little Book of Success
The Little Book of Yoga
The Magic of Forgiveness
The Miracle of Forgiving
The New Age Diet: Vegetarianism for You and Me

The Perfect Relationship: Guru and Disciple
The Terror Within
The Way of Abhyasa (How To Meditate)
Thus Have I Been Taught
Tips For Teenagers
What You Would Like To know About Karma
What You Would Like To know About Hinduism
What to Do When Difficulties Strike: 8 easy Practical Suggestions.
Why Do Good People Suffer?
Women: Where Would the World Be Without You
You Are Not Alone: God Is With You!
You Can Change Your Life: Live—Don't Just Exist!
Why Be Sad?

Story Books:

100 Stories You Will Never Forget
101 Stories For You And Me
25 Stories For Children and also for teens
Break the Habit
It's All A Matter of Attitude!
More Snacks For The Soul
Snacks for the Soul
The Heart of a Mother
The King of Kings
The Lord Provides
The Miracle of Forgiving
The One Thing Needful
The Patience of Purna
The Power of Good Deeds
The Power of Thought
Trust Me All in All or Not at All
Whom Do You Love the Most
You Can Make A Difference

Books and Booklets by J.P. Vaswani

In Hindi
Jiski Jholi Mein Hain Pyaar (Dada J.P. Vaswani His Life and Teachings)
Pyar Ka Masiha (Pilgrim of Love)
Sadhu Vaswani: Unkaa Jeevan Aur Shikshaayen (Sadhu Vaswani His Life and Teachings)
Aalwar Santon Ki Mahan Gaathaayen
Brindavan Ka Balak
Santon Ki Leela
Bhakton Ki Uljhanon Kaa Saral Upaai
Dainik Prerna (Daily Inspiration)
Krodh Ko Jalayen Swayam Ko Nahin (Burn Anger Before Anger Burns You)
Prarthna ki Shakti
Safal Vivah Ke Dus Rahasya (10 Commandments of a Successful Marriage)
Atmik Jalpaan (Snacks for the Soul)
Atmik Poshan (More Snacks for the Soul)
Bhale Logon Ke Saath Bura Kyon? (Why Do Good People Suffer?)
Mrutyu Hai Dwar . . . Phir Kya? (Life After Death)
Chahat Hai Mujhe Ik Teri Teri! (Hindi Booklet)
Ishwar Tujhe Pranam (Begin the Day with God)
Shama Karo, Sukhi Raho

In Marathi:
Krodhala Shaanth Kara, Krodhane Ghala Ghalnya Purveech (Burn Anger Before Anger Burns You)

Sufi Sant (Sufi Saints of East and West)
Jyachya Jholit Aahay Prem (Pilgrim of Love)
Mrutyu Nantar Che Jeevan (Life after Death)
Karma Mhanje Kay? Samjun Ghayaych? Karma (What You Would Like To Know About Karma)
Yashasvi Vyavahik Jeevanchi Sutre (10 Commandments of a Successful Marriage)

In Kannada:
Burn Anger Before Anger Burns You
Life After Death
Why do Good People Suffer
101 Stories For You And Me
Tips for Teenagers

In Telugu:
Life after Death
Burn Anger Before Anger Burns You
What You Would Like To Know About Karma

In Spanish:
Mas Respuestas de Dada (Dada Answers)
Todo es Cuestion de Actitud! (It's All A Matter of Attitude)
Mas Bocaditos Para el Alma (More Snacks for the Soul)
Bocaditos Para el Alma (Snacks for the Soul)
Inicia Tu Dia Con Dios (Begin the Day with God)
Cita Diario Con Dios (Daily Appointment with God!)
El Buen Cuidado De Las Hijos (Good Parenting)
L'Inspiration Quotidienne (Daily Inspiration)
Aprenda A Controlar Su Ira (Burn Anger Before Anger Burns You)
Queme La Ira Antes Que La Ira Lo Queme A Usted (Burn Anger Before Anger Burns You)
El Bein Quentu Hagas, Regresa (The Good You Do Returns)
Mata al miedo antes de que el miedo te mate (Kill Fear Before Fear Kills you)
Encontro Diario Com Deus (Daily Appontment With God)
Sita Diario ku Dios (I Luv U, God!)
Vida despu'es de la Muerte (Life After Death)
Mas Cerca Oh Dios De Ti! (Nearer My God To Thee)
Tiene Dios Favoritos? (Does God Have Favorites?)
Lo Que a Usted Legustaria Saber Sobre el Karma (What you would Like to Know about Karma)
101 Historias Paraa Ti Y Para Mi (101 Stories For You & Me)
Simplemente Vegetariano (Simply Vegetarian)
10 Mandamientos Para Un Exitoso Matrimonio (10 Commandments of Successful Marriage)

Books and Booklets by J.P. Vaswani

Maneje su Vida
  Momento a Momento
  (Management Moment
  By Moment)
Deje De Quejarse Y
  Empiece a Agradecer!
  (Stop Complaining
  Start Thanking)
Asi Nos Han Ensenado!
  (Thus I have been
  taught)
Tu Puedes Marcar La
  diferencia (You Can
  Make A Difference)

In Arabic:
Daily Appointment with
  God
Daily Inspiration
Thus Spake Sadhu
  Vaswani

In Chinese:
Daily Appointment With
  God

In Dutch:
Begin De Dag Met God
  (Begin The Day With
  God)

In Bahasa:
Life After Death

Musnahkan Kemarahan
  Sebelum Amarah
  Memusnahkan Anda
  (Burn Anger Before
  Anger Burns You)
A Little Book of Success
A Little Book of Wisdom
Menulis Di Atas Pasir
  (It's All A Matter of
  Attitude)

In Gujrati:
Its All A Matter of Attitude
Ishwar Se Dainik Bhet
  (Daily Appointment
  with God)
Life After Death
Flowers & Fruits

In Oriya:
Snacks For The Soul
More Snacks For the Soul
Why Do Good People
  Suffer
Burn Anger Before Anger
  Burns You
Pilgrim of Love
Life After Death
Prathna Ki Shakti

In Russian:
What would you like to
  Know about Karma
Burn Anger Before Anger
  Burns You

In Sindhi:
Why Do Good People
  Suffer
Burn Anger Before Anger
  Burns You

In Tamil:
Why Do Good People
  Suffer
Burn Anger Before Anger
  Burns You
Snacks For The Soul
Its All a Matter of Attitude
More Snacks For the Soul
Secrets of Health and
  Happiness
10 Commandments of a
  Successful Marriage
Kill Fear Before Fear Kills
  You
Daily Appointment with
  God

In Latvia:
The Magic of Forgiveness

In French:
Burn Anger Before Anger
  Burns You

Contents

1. The Fascinating Enigma of the Human Personality 1

2. Negative Traits in People 9

3. The Enemies Within 16

4. Pride, Ego and Arrogance 23

5. Prejudice, Intolerance and Hatred 32

6. Inferiority Complex 50

7. Laziness 61

8. The Failings of Excessive Desire:
   Lust, Greed and Gluttony 73

9. Envy and Jealousy 107

10. The Secret of an Integrated Personality 119

1

The Fascinating Enigma of the Human Personality

ᘒᕝᕗ ᕫᘓᕗ

Why did God create you and give you the great gift of the human birth?

The simple answer to that question is this: God is your loving father; He wants you to be happy; He wants to draw you closer to Him; and therefore, He bestowed on you this gift of the human birth.

God has made us in His image. He is perfect bliss. As His image, are we not also happiness personified? *Tat twam asi!* That art Thou! You are supreme joy and you are eternal bliss. It is only when you forget this that you lose your happiness. You forget your true nature. You forget that you are an aspect of the Divine. It is this lack of self-knowledge, this *avidya* that makes you unhappy.

A beautiful incident is narrated to us in the *Dnyandev Gatha* which recounts the life of Sant Dnyaneshwar. Dnyaneshwar and his sister Muktabai instructed young Namdev, who came to them as an aspirant, to journey the famous Shiva temple of Aundha Nagnath, where, they promised, he would find a Guru to initiate him on the path. Promptly, Namdev travelled to the temple, located in a dense forest. On entering the temple, he was horrified to see an ascetic, reclining with his feet on the sacred *Shiva linga.*

Namdev flew into a rage and shouted at the ascetic, "Are you blind? Or are you mad? How dare you place your feet on the sacred idol? What a sacrilege this is! Take your feet off and go and sleep elsewhere!"

The ascetic opened his eyes and smiled at Namdev. "I was expecting you to come to me," he said. "Now, let me see, shall I rest here . . . or here . . . why don't you move my feet wherever you think is proper?"

An irate Namdev dragged the ascetic's feet away from the *Linga.* To his amazement, wherever he placed the feet, a *Linga* sprang up! He fell at the feet of the ascetic, whose yogic powers had filled the temple with multiple *Lingas,* and sought his forgiveness.

The yogi, a disciple of Sant Dnayaneshwar, was none other than Visoba Khechar. He initiated the young Namdev into the mantra *Tat twam asi*—That art Thou! Thus Namdev was taught the Omnipresence of God, and His presence as the *antaryami* or indweller in us all.

With an unhappy mind, how can you look for happiness? How can you hope to find it outside, when your 'inside' is dark and clouded?

No matter who you are, no matter what circumstance you are placed in, you must realise that happiness is your birthright. You are entitled to happiness, and there are no 'conditions' to fulfill, no strings attached.

Unfortunately, most of us are engaged in searching the entire world over for happiness and fulfillment. If we search until our last breath, we are not going to find happiness 'out there somewhere'. We cannot wish for it; we cannot buy it; nobody can hand it over to us on a platter. It is a very personal feeling—and it must come from within!

Let me repeat: happiness does not depend on outer things. Happiness is essentially an inner quality! Happiness is your birthright! But happiness must come from within you!

You cannot depend on another person to make you happy or 'give' you happiness. This will place a tremendous strain on both of you. On the other hand, if you are truly happy inside yourself and allow the other person to feel the same, then both of you are truly bringing happiness to each other—without any expectations, without any pre-conditions, without any anticipations.

Always dream and shoot higher than you know you can do. Do not bother just to be better than your contemporaries or predecessors. Try to be better than yourself.

—William Faulkner

The Lord says to us in the Gita: Man can be his own best friend; he can also choose to be his own worst enemy!

The poet John Milton echoes this sentiment in these famous lines:

The mind is its own place; and in itself
Can make a Heaven of Hell, a Hell of Heaven.

Significantly, the lines come from his immortal epic, *Paradise Lost*. When your mind makes itself a veritable hell, filled, cluttered with undesirable, negative thoughts, you lose the paradise of happiness which is your birthright.

How many of us can honestly say we are happy?

From all available evidence, it would seem that true happiness is something of a rarity in the world today. In fact, many writers assert that unhappiness is the most prevalent feeling in the world now.

What are we going to do about it? How are we going to reclaim the happiness that is our birthright?

I have a simple suggestion: Let us begin with ourselves.

I am sure most of you will have read these beautiful lines somewhere:

> My mind to me a kingdom is;
> Such perfect joy therein I find
> That it excels all other bliss . . .

We are responsible for our own happiness, and the quest for that happiness which is our birthright must begin from within us!

What do you think you will find when you start looking within?

Why am I as I am? To understand that of any person, his whole life, from birth must be reviewed. All of our experiences fuse into our personality. Everything that ever happened to us is an ingredient.

—Malcolm X, The Autobiography Of
Malcolm X

The mind is an instrument of cognition, of knowing things, knowing the material world. The soul is a ray of God, 'that' which you essentially are. The mind is an instrument with which we know, with which we try to understand things. The mind is discursive, while the soul is synergic. While the soul integrates everything, the mind analyses everything.

We need the help of the mind in doing our work on the physical plane. That is why we have brought with ourselves the instrument of the mind. In your mind you have a friend who is with you 24-hours a day! You may be alone, helpless or in distress, but your mind is ever ready to help you and to guide you to overcome any situation. But it is up to you to *use* it in the right way.

I recommend 'shampooing' the mind everyday! We need to cleanse our mind, we need to unclutter our mind, which often gets filled with wrong thinking and wrong ideas. And, then, the minds of so many of us are negative. We must cleanse the mind of all the dirt and negativity that we have accumulated over the years. To do this, we must get right down into our consciousness and shampoo away all the rotten negativities that hold us captive—negativities like impurity, selfishness, greed, lust and hatred, and oh, so many more!

The human psyche is indeed a marvellous thing. Its profoundity, its complexity and its capability are yet to be fully understood by us, or utilised to its optimum capacity. Let me quote the words of Hamlet, the Prince of Denmark:

> What a piece of work is a man, how noble in reason, how infinite in faculties, in form and moving how express and admirable, in action how like an angel, in apprehension how like a God! The beauty of the world, the paragon of animals . . .

Nobility, grace, reason, blessed with many skills and abilities, mastery over movement and beauty of form and face and figure—along with that great cognitive instrument, the mind, which makes him the crown of creation! What does man lack?

"Principally I hate and detest that animal called man," wrote the essayist and satirist, Jonathan Swift. Difficult to believe, is it not, that Shakespeare and Swift are talking about the same species—*homo sapiens* as we are called!

> We prefer to go deformed and distorted all our lives rather than not resemble the portrait of ourselves which we ourselves have first drawn. It's absurd. We run the risk of warping what's best in us.
>
> —André Gide

Ancient philosophers regarded man as a composite of three levels of nature—the divine, the human and the bestial. Or, to put it differently, as a creature who could rise to the level of the spiritual, function at the level of the physical, or be dragged down to the level of the senses and the passions. In simple terms, we understand this to mean that human beings are a combination of both positive and negative energy. We draw closer to the Divine in us, in the measure in which we are able to overcome the negative energies in us. For what is Divinity, but the complete absence of all negative forces?

Negative energy is generated by negative emotions, which drag us down and cause unhappiness—to us and others. Constant pressure from negative emotions can actually distort our personality and our life and deprive us of our birthright— true happiness. Conquering these negative tendencies then, is the secret of inner joy and peace. At the start and end of each day, we must be able to see ourselves in the mirror, and like what we see therein we must be at peace in the heart within; we must go to sleep and awaken with a clear conscience; we must face up to our innermost thoughts and feelings and not be filled with self-loathing or contempt for what we think and feel and do . . .

There are very many negative emotions that cause an imbalance in our lives, like jealousy, anger, envy, greed, sloth, shame, guilt, etc. Not only do they disrupt our energy system, but also lead to mental and physical disorders.

How can we conquer these negative tendencies? How may we arrest the negative energies that rob us of true joy and contentment and restore our own positive self-image? How can we live our precious life as well-balanced, mature individuals?

Let us explore the choices before us in the pages that follow.

PRACTICAL TIP:

Experts recommend four ways to overcome stress and tension and increase the Happiness Quotient:

1. Reserve for yourself at least fifteen minutes of PQT (personal quiet time) during the day to reflect, introspect and talk to yourself on positive living.

2. Rediscover the beautiful habit of reading. Read at least twenty pages of a classic, a great masterpiece or inspirational literature every day. If you decide to turn to the scriptures for daily reading, that would be better than everything else!

3. Reconnect with good friends who share your spiritual/emotional vibrations. The world was not meant to be a lonely planet!

4. Do something creative. Rediscover the fine art of hobbies. Sing, dance or paint your heart out!

2
Negative Traits in People

───── ༀ ༃ ──────

Some years ago, a group of people decided to conduct a survey on, "What I hate about myself". They mailed questionnaires to people asking them to fill them and deposit the filled-in forms at a library—with or without filling in their names and addresses. To their surprise, not only did they receive a lot of responses, but also found that people did not shy away from revealing their identity or show any reluctance to discuss what they perceived to be their negative traits with others.

What were some of the things that people hated most about themselves? Given below are a few answers:

1. I am rude to people
2. I expect everyone to love me and treat me well but I can't do the same for others
3. I judge people harshly
4. I pretend to be good, but only to show off to people; in reality, I am not as good as I make out to be
5. I am never satisfied—with what I am, what I have or what I eat
6. I am always getting into debt
7. I hate myself

8. I can't face trouble

9. I find fault with everything and everyone

10. I am too lazy to make anything of my life

And the list went on and on . . .

I must add here, that I think the people who responded to the questionnaire were honest to themselves and to others, in facing up to their own negative traits. After all, we often use the term, 'the dark side of human nature' to refer to those traits that people prefer not to talk about. Many of us have flaws and weaknesses which we hide from others; some of us prefer not to face up to them ourselves; we actually refuse to see the truth about ourselves. That is why I expressed my admiration for the people who actually subjected themselves to a self-analysis, and were aware of their own weaknesses. After all, it has been said that it is the worst man who sees himself as the best—that is, he is unaware of his own flaws and weaknesses.

An animal activist (rather, a great lover of the animal kingdom) once said to me that he greatly resented the way animal traits were often used to describe human tendencies such as violence, aggression, cruelty and selfishness; according to him, NHAs or non-human animals were far less aggressive and cruel than the human animals; but he also added that it is not human nature that is flawed, but human behaviour and conduct that is, occasionally, 'dark' and 'flawed'.

That is an interesting observation: for we are yet to fathom the causes, the reasons for the way human beings think, act and feel. What is it that makes us selfish, greedy or jealous? Why are some of us prone to inferiority complex? What makes people suicidal? What are the causes, the origins and the characteristics of these tendencies? Are these traits inherent, inborn or acquired from the human environment? These are some of the most discussed issues in human psychology.

Some psychologists contend that human beings are inherently prone to evil; while others argue that our deepest longing is to be socially and morally attuned with the rest of our fellow human beings.

Perhaps the truth is that man has the potential to be both good and evil. To quote Viktor Frankl, a psychologist and a survivor of the Nazi concentration camps, "Our generation has come to know man as he really is. He is the being who invented the gas chambers of Auschwitz. He is also the being who entered those gas chambers with a prayer on his lips."

God gave us the freedom of will to exercise our choice: it is our choices that determine what kind of people we are. Ernest Valea, a scholar of comparative religions tells us: "The general pattern in Eastern religions is to consider evil as the effect of spiritual ignorance . . . According to Christianity, evil is neither created nor a natural or necessary element. It is a parasite state that perpetuates itself by misusing God's good resources and by following a wrong direction. It is the illness of beings that are no longer in communion with God."

One thing is obvious: just as darkness is absence of light, evil is absence of goodness. Just as a tiny lamp can dispel darkness, so too, the assertion of good can destroy the negative tendencies in us. Therefore, we have the choice to conquer the negative traits that lead to unhappiness, evil or sin; all we have to do is to choose the positives, choose good, choose God.

It has always seemed strange to me . . . the things we admire in men, kindness and generosity, openness, honesty, understanding and feeling, are the concomitants of failure in our system. And those traits we detest, sharpness, greed, acquisitiveness, meanness, egotism and self-interest, are the traits of success. And while men admire the quality of the first they love the produce of the second.

—John Steinbeck

I have always believed that within each one of us, there are two selves: the lower self and the higher self. The lower self is the self of passion and pride, lust and hatred, greed, resentment and ill-will, jealousy and envy. All these base passions go to make up the lower self. May I tell you what our problem is? It is that many of us have identified ourselves with this lower self of the passions. It is also called the ego-self, which sits on the threshold of our consciousness. It easily catches us, captures our attention, misleads us, and leads us astray on the path of evil and negativity. Trapped in its power, we are struggling in the darkness which is our own shadow. This is the tragedy of modern man, that he has identified himself with this lower self!

Let me say to you, this lower self may dominate us often; but it is a tiny pathetic thing! When we sit in meditation or enter into the depths within ourselves, we will realise that this lower self is nothing but the speck of the speck of a speck! It is so petty! And yet, in our daily life, we magnify it out of all proportion! We think of it as our own true self. We allow it to dominate our thoughts and actions. We go to it again and again, and submit to its dictates. We follow its impulses like obedient servants; that is why we have amongst us, thieves, frauds, forgers, fakes, criminals, liars and murderers! That is why the world today is rocked by wars, violence, hatred, strife, intolerance and prejudice. All these negativities are the outcome of the baser emotions, of man's lower self in ascendancy.

But this lower self is only a part of the story of man—in fact, it is less than a fraction! For within each one of us is a higher self—the true self which the Gita refers to as the *atman*. Each one of us is the *atman*—the indestructible, eternal self, the self of utter truth and bliss that we call *sat chit ananda!* There have been, there are, and there will continue to be amongst us, realised souls who will always remain our guides, guardians, mentors and teachers who will persistently and untiringly show the way forward, the way onward, the way Godward to the rest of us. These are people who have realised their Oneness with the Supreme Self.

This is what we are in reality, the highest self, which is a spark of the Supreme Self.

He who knows no hardships will know no hardihood. He who faces no calamity will need no courage. Mysterious though it is, the characteristics in human nature which we love best grow in a soil with a strong mixture of troubles.

—Harry Emerson Fosdick

A friend once said to me, "Dada, if we are imperfect, it is because God has willed it, ordained it to be so. Why should we fight against what He has ordained? Why should we try to become perfect, flying in the face of Providence?"

I responded to his question with a story. A lazy man once approached an honest labourer and said to him, "Please give me some money. I cannot work, and I am starving."

The labourer said to him, "I can see that you are able-bodied and fit. Why don't you work for a living as all of us do? Why do you go around begging?"

"It is my nature to be lazy and poor," the beggar replied. "How can I change my nature?"

Obviously, the working man was not satisfied with this reply.

The truth is that we are all here to put forth our best efforts. The ideal before each one of us must be the ideal of perfection. We would do well to remind ourselves of Jesus's words: "Be ye perfect, even as your Father in Heaven is perfect." In order to strive towards this ideal of perfection, which, incidentally, is the goal of human life, we have to conquer the lower self. We have to conquer our base desires and the lower passions and walk the way of self-control and self-discipline. The alternative is to slip into the role of the lazy beggar—unable, unwilling to improve our condition by our own effort.

Each one of us is a child of God. God, as we know, is the King of kings. Does this not make each one of us a prince or a princess? We must always live in this awareness. We are princes and princesses; and there are some things that a royal personage would never ever do! This awareness will keep us away from our baser self and its domination.

I believe this is the purpose of religion: to put us in touch with our highest selves. *Tat twam asi!* That art Thou! These were the words of our great rishis. You are not a worm, a pathetic creature crawling between birth and death. You are That! Once you realise this truth, the lower self is conquered, and the highest in you begins to assert itself. All you have to do, is connect to your higher self, connect to God, and all negativities vanish, as mist before the morning sun!

PRACTICAL TIP:

Eight Steps To Interior Peace

1. Begin the day with God
2. Let your mind constantly return to God
3. Stop worrying—and let God take over your problems
4. Don't dwell on problems—dwell on solutions
5. Count your blessings
6. Accept God's Will
7. Do your best—and leave the rest to God
8. Make prayer a habit

3

The Enemies Within

Gurudev Sadhu Vaswani was often asked how he could advocate reverence for all life and *ahimsa* as absolute ideals, when the Hindu scriptures themselves supported animal sacrifice in *yagnas*. His answer was both simple and straightforward: "The soul of India," he declared, "has never countenanced the killing of creatures . . . when the *Vedas* speak of sacrifice, they refer to the internal sacrifice, the sacrifice of self-seeking impulses, the sacrifice of the animal within us . . . the sacrifice or *bali* of *kama, krodha* and the passions . . ."

May I add, the literal meaning of the word *yagna* is sacrifice. But it is the sacrifice of the ego and the animals within us that true *yagna* calls for! It is this that makes possible true inner cleansing which is the first step towards self-realisation. The *yagna*, in its truest sense, is a form of worship that is essentially spiritual in practice. The whole concept of animal sacrifice is thus deeply symbolic, asking us to sacrifice or destroy in the fire of the spirit, all that is base and ignoble within us! For these are the enemies within, which constitute impediments on the path of self-realisation, self fulfillment and achieving the true joy of life.

Our scriptures use a special term to refer to these impediments: the *shada ripus* or six enemies within each one of us: *Kama* (lust), *Krodha* (anger), *Lobha* (greed), *Moha* (delusion), *Mada* (egoistic tendencies) and *Matsarya* (jealousy).

We are ever ready to blame other people, external factors, circumstances, fate, fortune, at times even the Good Lord Himself for our unhappiness, problems and failures. But the truth is that we are responsible for our own lives, and it is time we became accountable to ourselves: thus the need to conquer the enemies within!

In Christian parlance, there is mention of "seven deadly sins" that are similar to the *shada ripus*: wrath, greed, sloth, pride, lust, envy and gluttony. Buddhism too, talks of the three main roots of evil, called *mula priyaya* in Pali, which are anger, greed and delusion or ignorance: *lobha, dosha, moha*. In Pali, these terms are closely interlinked; *lobha* is greed, desire, attachment; *dosha* is anger, hatred, hostility, aversion; *moha* is delusion, ignorance, lack of true knowledge. Enlightenment must replace delusion: the enemies within must be conquered.

Early in my life, I learnt the truth that we are not punished *for* our sins, but *by* our sins; that is, we suffer because of our failings, our weaknesses which are largely inner failures. What some people regard as sins, are essentially inner weaknesses which we can actually conquer, if we are willing to 'kill' the animals within! I think it is only because people were unwilling to take on this task of self-conquest that the barbaric practice of animal sacrifice came into vogue. Can I burn the anger within me? Difficult! How much easier to slaughter an innocent creature instead? Can I swallow my ego and arrogance? Far simpler to sacrifice a goat or chicken and swallow its flesh as *prasad!* Perhaps this is how animal sacrifice came into vogue.

I cannot help thinking that the demons and evil forces depicted so powerfully in our epics and *puranas* are also symbolic representations of these negative forces, the enemies within, as we refer to them. In this sense, the Ramayana and Mahabharata are actually being enacted in the daily lives of us all! Ravana is nothing but a personification of the enemies within us—such as ego, lust, covetousness, envy and pride. The Kurukshetra war is nothing but a metaphorical representation of the good and evil that is present within each one of us.

Conquering the enemies within is not a one-time battle in which you or I can emerge an all-time winner. It is a way of life, a mode of conduct, a discipline which we impose on ourselves to achieve the happiness that is our birthright as children of God.

Whenever I hear people say that happiness is impossible to achieve in *kaliyuga*, I think to myself that it is the enemies within that have become difficult to conquer in the present generation! In this sense, this book is as much about dealing with our negative traits, as it is about victory over the self!

But help is at hand for us if we wish to conquer these enemies within:

1. Pray to God for His special grace: He is all kindness, all compassion, He is the origin and source of all that is good and positive and wholesome. When you acknowledge that He is your Father and Mother, you live in the awareness that you are God's child and He will do only what is best for you.

2. Seek the guidance of a Guru, a spiritual mentor. You will hear this from me again and again; believe me, it is worth repeating! Spending time in the presence of an evolved soul is the most powerful source of strength and inner wisdom. A Guru inspires us by his living example. He sees the potential in us that we ourselves are not aware of. Above all he encourages us to believe that we are also capable of achieving what he has! He provides tremendous powers of incentive and inspiration. He cures us of crippling negative emotions. In this human birth, we cannot see God in person; but it is our good fortune that we can see the Guru, hear his *upadesh*, associate ourselves with daily *satsang*, accept his gracious *prasad*—indeed, grasp his holy feet

firmly—and through him, all God's blessings and all God's grace will come to us!

A Guru inspires us by his living example. He sees the potential in us that we ourselves are not aware of. He provides tremendous power of incentive and inspiration and cures us of crippling negative emotions.

As the seeker proceeds on the path, he must never forget that he is always under the umbrella of his Guru.

The Guru is the great protector.

—J. P. Vaswani

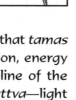

3. Cultivate self-discipline. The Gita teaches us that *tamas* is overcome by *rajas*—the principle of action, energy and dynamism. When we cultivate discipline of the mind, it will automatically lead us to *sattva*—light and harmony. With this enlightenment, our spiritual progress can be really speedy. Offer all that you are, all that you have, all that you do, to the Lord, in a spirit of surrender—a spirit of *arpanam*.

4. Sri Krishna tells us in the Gita: "Whatever you eat, whatever you give in charity, whatever austerity you practise, whatever you do, O Arjuna, make it as an offering unto Me." This is the best antidote to conquering the ego, negating pride and arrogance, and conquering those enemies within. Whatever you do, offer it to God. Whatever you achieve, it is His grace, His doing. Therefore say to Him: "I am not the doer. I am but a broken instrument. If there are any shortcomings, any mistakes that I make, they are mine. But all glory belongs to Thee!"

Letting The Tiger Loose

Our puranas narrate the story of a poor peasant who was walking through a thick forest. All of a sudden, he heard the most plaintive moans coming from a dark thicket. On approaching the location, he saw a tiger locked up in an iron cage. The animal actually had tears flowing from its eyes, and in a pathetic vein, called out to the peasant, "O, dear brother! Have pity on me and let me out. I am wounded and in great pain; I am famished and also very, very thirsty."

The peasant was awestruck at the sight of the ferocious animal pleading with him so pathetically. But he said, with great fear, "If I let you out of the cage, you will eat me." The tiger replied, "How could you think so badly of me? I would never ever be so ungrateful. Please let me out; I will bless you and go my way and leave you alone. How could I ever dream of harming a benefactor?"

The peasant was moved to pity, and opened the cage door to let him out. No sooner was the animal out of the cage, he sprang against the unsuspecting peasant and roared, "Prepare to die, you foolish man! Now I will eat you!"

The peasant was appalled. "How could you go back on your word?" he cried, running around in circles, desperately trying to save himself. "How could you be so ungrateful? I was the one who gave you freedom, and you will eat me?" The tiger said, "You knew I was a wounded tiger. What did you expect? You surely deserve to die for your folly!"

At that moment, a holy man who happened to be passing by, heard the commotion and came to investigate the matter. The peasant fell at his feet and implored the sage to save his life. As for the tiger, it said to the holy man, "O, wise one! You know that I must live according to my nature. Will you deny me my legitimate prey?"

The holy man said to them, "First let me hear what you both are arguing about." The peasant narrated the incident to him and asked him whether it was fair on the tiger's part to attack him thus.

The sage listened carefully and answered, "Look, I cannot really decide on the rights and wrongs of this matter unless I know exactly what happened right from the beginning. Where were you? Where was the tiger?"

The peasant said, "I was passing by when I heard his pathetic moans. I found him locked in the cage and he begged me to release him."

"Is that so?" said the holy man. "And where were you?" he said, turning to the tiger. "Inside the cage", said the tiger. "Was the cage locked and bolted?" asked the sage. "Yes," replied the tiger.

The sage looked at the cage for a moment and said, "You are lying! How is it possible for a tiger your size to fit in such a small cage?" The tiger was in a hurry to get a decision from the sage, so he jumped back in the cage and said, "See for yourself!" Thereupon, the holy man promptly locked the cage and said, "You are a wicked and ungrateful animal, and this is where you belong! You can stay there for the rest of your days!"

The peasant thanked the holy man from the bottom of his heart for saving his life and they both went their way, happily.

Moral: This simple fable teaches us a valuable lesson: the tiger represents the six foes of a man (shadripu). If they are not kept under control they can destroy a man.

ঙ্গ ঙ্গ

PRACTICAL TIP:

Rate yourself on each of the following traits.
Put the number from the rating scale which most accurately
describes the trait in you.

{Rating scale: 0 = never; 1 = seldom; 2 = sometimes;
3 = often; 4 = usually}

Argumentative _____	Harsh _____
Arrogant _____	Hateful _____
Bitter _____	Hostile _____
Blame-shifting _____	Hypocritical _____
Blowup _____	Impatient _____
Brash _____	Impractical _____
Brutal _____	Inconsiderate _____
Indifferent _____	Indecisive _____
Closeminded _____	Greedy _____
Complaining _____	Inflexible _____
Conceited _____	Insensitive _____
Covetous _____	Insulting _____
Critical _____	Interfering _____
Cruel _____	Irresponsible _____
Deceitful _____	Jealous _____
Demanding _____	Judgmental _____
Disobedient _____	Lazy _____
Domineering _____	Lordly _____
Embarrassing _____	Lying _____
Get the last word _____	Manipulating _____
Malicious _____	Nagging _____
Gossipy _____	

Pick up any one trait with the score of 3 or 4 and with the
blessings of your Guru and your own determined efforts try
to reduce the score to 0 or 1 in a few months.

ঙ্গ ঙ্গ

4

Pride, Ego and Arrogance

Holy men and sages tell us that humility is the true mark of the evolving soul; and humility is not easy to attain—for it involves the utter effacement of the ego.

Alas, for many of us, I'm afraid, the ego is unconquerable. Man has conquered space; man has conquered the sky; man has even managed to control the courses of the rivers and the growth of the great forests—but man has not found it easy to control or conquer the ego.

The Dictionary definition with which we usually begin, tells us that egoism is, "an inflated feeling of pride in your superiority to others." When egoism manifests itself in outward behaviour, it becomes arrogance: "Overbearing pride evidenced by a superior manner toward inferiors."

As for pride, it can be something positive, a sense of self-worth, a feeling of self-respect. Excessive pride of course becomes ruinous to a good life: it is "unreasonable and inordinate self-esteem" (personified as one of the deadly sins denounced by Christianity.)

The sad truth today is that pride is no longer the prerogative of the high and mighty, the rich and powerful. The common man today has acquired the sins of haughtiness, arrogance, conceit, excessive pride and vanity. As a popular preacher puts it: "The sin of pride is responsible for so much of the confusion, sorrow, heartache and tragedy in our world today." She adds: "The middle letter in pride is 'I' just as 'I' is the middle letter in sin. Therefore self is at the heart of all sin; for sin is centered around 'I': I must have my pleasure; I must have my way; I must have everything my heart desires no matter what it costs me or others."

According to the Bible, pride in its various guises is an evidence that we are living in the last days of the earth, as we are told in II Tim. 3:2,4: "Men shall be lovers of their own selves . . . boasters, proud . . . heady, highminded."

St. Augustine of Hippo wrote, "Pride is the commencement of all sins because it was this which overthrew the devil, from whom arose the origin of sin; and afterwards, when his malice and envy pursued man, who was yet standing in his uprightness, it subverted him in the same way in which he himself fell. For the serpent, in fact, only sought for the door of pride whereby to enter when he said, 'Ye shall be as gods.'"

The *asuras* or demons are standing examples of overwheening pride and arrogance in Hindu mythology. Without exception, each one of the major demons like Hiranya Kashipu, Ravana, Narakasura and Kansa presumes that he is invincible and that no power on earth or in heaven can destroy him. The curious thing we learn about some of them is that they often put themselves through tough physical and spiritual austerities and offered their entire being to Gods like Brahma and Shiva to attain this invincibility: what we must note is that their spiritual disciplines and *sadhanas* failed to rid them of their ego and pride!

Let us therefore take note, that spiritual pride is as much a sin as physical or material pride! Who are we to assume that our piety, prayer and *sadhana* make us superior to others? On the contrary, they should teach us the virtue of humility and make us realise that we are all dependent on God's grace and it is His mercy and kindness that helps us against all odds!

A farmer and his young son went into the wheat fields at harvest time. As they looked across the waving fields of golden grain, the boy exclaimed, "Look, Father, at those wheat heads that hold themselves up so proudly. They must be the ones that are filled with grain, and I would suppose that those with their heads bowed are of no account."

"How foolish you are, my son!" the farmer said, and taking some of the heads in his hands, he showed the boy that the heads that stood up so proudly had only a few, poor, shriveled grains or were complete empty, while those that bowed their heads humbly were filled with large, full, golden kernels of wheat.

What causes the negative traits of arrogance/pride/ ego? It is the presence of unconscious *vasanas* (subtle desires) in the mind which give rise to ego. Most of our human interactions are based on the ego. In fact, for the vast majority of the people, their ego is their identity. When people are disgruntled or disappointed, their ego begins to rise like high fever. They try to assert themselves, to assert their self-will, their ego. Little do they realise that ego only blocks the flow of energy and power into their lives!

When ego becomes the source of your motivation and initiative, you can achieve little; but when the ego is subdued, your higher self becomes the source of your advancement and initiative. This is what makes the best human achievements possible!

How can we conquer the ego? This is only done through constant *sadhana* (discipline) and the complete integration of one's personality. When you have reached this state, you will find that the best in you finds expression—your best qualities and talents are unfolded.

Alas, for most of us in the modern age, complete relaxation of the ego is achieved only during the sleeping state! Ego is then set aside, *not* by a process of conscious effort, but by a biological, unconscious process. This is why we say, "He/she is sleeping peacefully as a child."

When you are able to set aside your ego by a conscious voluntary effort, through your own intuition and understanding, you have taken the first step on the path of liberation and enlightenment. Of such a man, Chaitanya Mahaprabhu says—

> One who is humbler
> Than a blade of grass
> And yet, more enduring than a tree:
> One who gives respect to those who lack it—
> Such a devotee is fit to sing
> The praises of the Lord at all times!

Many distinguished scientists have said that when man realises the vastness, the grandeur and the immensity of the universe we live in, and our own insignificance in the universal scheme of things, it is impossible for us to feel egotistical and proud. Just think—at one time, the universe existed; time existed; creation existed; but planet earth did not exist; the solar system did not exist; man did not exist; and, in course of time, a day will come when this earth will cease to exist; and the solar system would have disintegrated. And yet, time will live on . . .

Peter the Great of Russia had a big idea to improve Russia, which was then in a backward state compared with the rest of Europe. So he left his exalted position, became first an apprentice, then a skilled workman, and finally a teacher and demonstrator. He worked as a shipbuilder in Holland and also at Deptford in England. He studied military science in Austria. The result was St. Petersburg, whose name has since been restored, which was founded by him. It rises out of the marshes, the capital and harbour for merchant ships, many of which Peter himself piloted in.

Of what are we proud, I often ask myself. Power, wealth, fame, youth, beauty—all, all are transient. As great ones have continually demonstrated, even world conquerors leave this earth empty-handed. Sant Dadu Dayal tells us—

When one lost what was one's own, and abandoned all pride of birth: when vain-glory has dropped away, then, only then, is one face to face with the Creator.

It was the great Sufi saint Rumi, who said: "When thou thyself shall come to be, then the beloved Lord wilt thou find. Therefore, O wise man, try to lose thyself, and feel humility." He adds, for further emphasis, "Egoism and self-will are opposed to the Holy Name; the two cannot dwell in the same house. None can serve the Lord without humility; the self-willed mind is worthless."

Humility does not consist in hiding our talents and virtues, or in thinking of ourselves as being worse than we really are; but in realising that all that we are, and all that we have, are freely given to us by God. Therefore, as Thomas a Kempis tells us, one of the best ways to acquire humility is to fix the following maxim in our mind: One is worth what he is worth in the eyes of God.

King Canute, a Danish conqueror of Britain, was one day flattered by his courtiers on account of his power. Then he ordered his throne to be placed by the seaside. The tide was rolling in, and threatened to drown him. He commanded the waves to stop. Of course, they did not. Then he said to his flatterers, "Behold, how small is the might of kings!"

I remember vividly an incident which occured when I was a child. I was doing my Geography homework one evening when a family friend walked into our house. His conversation was always loud. That day he began to boast about the row of buildings which he owned in Karachi.

"They occupy almost the whole street!" he asserted.

In my innocence and simplicity I went up to him with my atlas and said, "Uncle, will you be kind enough to point out your row of buildings on this map of India?"

Our friend was nonplussed. Karachi was indicated on the map by just a dot. How on earth could he mark out his row of buildings on that dot?

Guru Gobind Singh tells us:

> Emperors before whom strong armed kings did meekly bow their heads in countless numbers:
> Who possessed great elephants with golden trappings, proud and painted with brilliant colours:
> Millions of horses swifter than the wind which bounded o'er the world:
> What mattered it how mighty were these emperors?
> All at the last went hence
> With nothing, bare of foot.

Surely, our ancient rishis were right when they said: "*I and mine are the greatest obstacles on the Godward path.*"

Ego affects human relationships negatively:

- People with excessive egoism do not care to listen to their partners. This leads to a failure of communication and misunderstanding becomes habitual among friends and partners.
- An egotistical person fails to see his own mistakes. He assumes that he can never be wrong. This causes frustration and irritation among others.
- Mutual adjustments, a sense of give-and-take is vital to nourishing a relationship. Ego does not allow people to 'compromise' on their position, and this is ruinous to friendship and marriage.

- Excessive ego, the sense of superiority and arrogance result in domination and oppression. This is often cited as the major cause of divorce.

My Gurudev, Sadhu Vaswani, described the way of love, the way of devotion, as "the little way". To tread the "little way" he said, one had to be as humble as dust, realise one's nothingness, to 'lose' oneself, so that one could find God. These are his beautiful words from the Nuri Granth, a compilation of his immortal songs of devotion:

> What art thou?
> A mere nothing!
> Casting aside vestures of vanity,
> Live as a lowly one!
> In this speck of a universe,
> Thou art but a tiny speck:
> Why, then, art thou Puffed up with pride?
> Thou art but an insect:
> Yet is thy head
> Inflated with arrogance!

Ahankara—the ego—is an abyss; it is the pit of pride, the pit of darkness, where dwells Satan, Gurudev taught us.

It is with deliberate intention that I mention Gurudev Sadhu Vaswani here: for, as Swami Sivananda tells us, "Guru-Bhakti Yoga is the surest and best *sadhana* to destroy arrogance and to dissolve the vicious ego." He compares arrogance and pride to deadly pests that ruin the harvest of our life; and the best 'germicide' to destroy *avidya* and *ahankara* (ignorance and pride), according to him, is this unique and peerless Guru-Bhakti Yoga. These pests and deadly germs become quite powerless to "afflict the fortunate soul who saturates himself with the spirit of Guru-Bhakti Yoga. Blessed indeed is the man who earnestly takes to this Yoga," Swami Sivananda adds, "for he will obtain crowning success in all other Yogas. To him will accrue the choicest fruits of perfection in *Karma, Bhakti, Dhyana* and *Jnana*."

How can we dislodge the ego from the position of sovereignty and supremacy that it has occupied in our lives?

Let me offer you a few practical suggestions:

1. When you are with your friends, do not attempt to show off, or push yourself forward.

2. Avoid talking too much; the more you talk, the more you tend to monopolise conversation, and draw attention to yourself, feeding your own ego. It will do you immense good to remain silent and hear others talk.

3. Talk little to those you wish to help; what really helps is not your words, but your vibrations.

4. Always steer clear of the desire to tell others of your life and achievements, your experiences, your views and opinions; live and grow in the thought that you are not the ultimate authority on any subject.

5. Realise that your true value lies not in your outer, empirical self, but your inner imperishable self.

6. Cultivate friendship with this inner self. And meditate on the significant words of the Gita:

> He who hath conquered
> His lower self of cravings and desires,
> He hath his supreme friend found
> In the self, immortal, true!
> But he who's still a victim
> To his appetites and passions,
> Verily, the self becometh to him
> Hostile as an enemy!

Conquer the ego—so that your own 'self' does not become your enemy!

PRACTICAL TIP:

Learn to give compliments. Compliment at least three people today. In appreciating others, you too will be appreciated amply. Though simple, this exercise yields rich dividends! However, avoid the danger of insincere compliments.

5

Prejudice, Intolerance and Hatred

I have clubbed these three negative emotions together, because I believe they are different degrees, different shades of an attitude that, if unchecked, will lead to absolute hatred.

Prejudice is defined as, "a preconceived opinion not based on reason or experience". It often leads to dislike, hostility or unjust behaviour formed on such a basis: thus we have prejudice against foreigners, prejudice against people of a different faith or even prejudice against people who are not 'like us', whatever that means! It is an adverse judgement or opinion formed about someone beforehand, without knowledge of the facts concerning the person; as a preconceived opinion, it leads to an irrational hostile attitude, fear or even hatred towards a particular group, race or religion; it is an attitude of intolerance which may actually cause damage by generating fear or hatred.

Ask yourself: what happens when a person dislikes another for no good reason, or has formed a hostile opinion of someone before even getting to know them? We refuse to give the other person a chance: we prejudge him and our attitude to him hardens to such an extent, that he cannot be right, can say or do nothing right in our eyes.

When we are prejudiced, we tend to become intolerant, we make a judgment about an individual or group of individuals on the basis of their social, physical or cultural characteristics. Needless to say this only leads to strife and negative results.

In 1946, a well known researcher called Hartley conducted a study in the US. Respondents were asked about their attitudes concerning a variety of ethnic groups, including "Danireans", "Pirraneans", and "Wallonians". The study found that those people who were antagonistic towards blacks and Jews were also antagonistic toward these other three groups. The catch is that none of the three groups exist! This suggests that causes of prejudice can be found in the characteristics of those who are prejudiced by nature.

One can argue that a prejudiced opinion may also refer to a preconceived *favourable* opinion: for example, we often tend to be favourably disposed towards anyone who speaks our language, or comes from our part of the country. This kind of 'positive' predisposition is also called a bias towards something or someone. But we are talking about negative traits here, and it is usually adverse or detrimental to harmony between people and groups.

In fact, I would not be wrong if I were to say that prejudice/intolerance that culminates in hatred is responsible for many of the evils that beset the world today, such as communalism, casteism, strife and terrorism.

Think of Hitler's mass murder of innocent Jewish men, women and children: did he have any real, reasonable grounds to complain against them? He only fanned the flame of prejudice against them by accusing them falsely and spreading malicious gossip against them. He actually made intelligent Germans believe that all their problems—economic, social and political—would be solved if Jews were 'exterminated'. The resulting genocide perpetrated by the Third Reich was one of the ugliest episodes in world history.

"Man is burning," the Buddha repeated emphatically. "Some are trapped in the fire of hatred; others in the flames of envy, passion, greed or jealousy, ego and pride. Quench the flames! Quench the flames!"

Think of the inhuman practices perpetrated under the barbaric slave trade of the eighteenth and nineteenth centuries. How could men presume that people with a different skin colour were created to be exploited by others, sold as commodities and treated as sub-human species by so-called civilised races?

What causes people to become prejudiced? Psychologists suggest several reasons:

1. Prejudice and intolerance are often associated with a certain personality type—namely the authoritarian type. Their prejudice, it is said, meets certain inherent needs of their personality type. They need scapegoats; they need people whom they can blame indiscriminately; prejudice comes in handy.

2. Prejudice is also associated with ethnocentricism—the tendency to regard one's own community/ race/ nationality as superior, as being the 'norm'.

3. Sometimes, prejudice may arise from people's family environment. Parents who are cold, aloof, strict disciplinarians with strong views, may give rise to prejudice in their children.

4. Contrary to general perception, conservatism is not always associated with prejudice. Many conservatives adhere to tradition and custom; but they are not all

prejudiced against those who do not follow their values. On the other hand, many so-called liberals tend to be intolerant towards those whom they perceive as being 'orthodox'.

5. Like the family, the social environment can also lead to prejudiced attitudes; and these are imbibed throughout the changing phases of one's life.

6. Powerful media like TV and cinema can also inculcate prejudice in people. For example, generations of "Wild West' movies portrayed whites as saviours while Native American Indians were depicted as 'bad guys'. This leads to stereotyping of a whole community.

It is generally felt that the more educated an individual is, the less prejudiced he is likely to be. But this may also happen because educated people know how to be 'politically correct' in speech and behaviour.

An individual who is intolerant and prejudiced may exhibit the following negative behaviour traits:

1. Aggression
2. Superstition
3. Frustration
4. Hot temper
5. Rigidity in belief and thinking
6. Cynicism

Modern scholars call it fear of 'the other'—prejudice against, even hatred of people who are not like us—people with a different colour of skin, people speaking a different language, people professing a different faith are not to be trusted; worse, they are actively targeted and vilified.

We talk of the world shrinking and becoming a global village; indeed, all of us are only too eager to buy and sell, carry on business with all corners of the globe, but underneath, deep distrust and prejudice prevails.

Colonisation may be a thing of the past—but economic and political hegemony prevails in other and more subtler forms.

'Foreigners' are treated with suspicion—especially those belonging to 'other' races and religions.

Strangers who talk differently and dress differently are subject to being treated as criminals or terrorists. If you don't like the look of your fellow-passenger on a flight, you can actually 'off load' him like a piece of luggage.

And we are used to speaking in glowing terms about something called, 'The Brotherhood of Man'!

Talking of Europe and America, let us not forget that we in India have also been guilty of such prejudice and exploitation: casteism, communalism and exploitation of women have been blots on our culture and civilisation!

My Gurudev, Sadhu Vaswani, described the principle of *karma* as the principle of a boomerang. What you send, comes back to you! Do you gossip about another? You will be gossiped about!

Do you send out thoughts of hatred and enmity to another? Hatred and enmity will come back to you, turning your life into a veritable hell! Do you send out loving thoughts to others? Do you pray for struggling souls? Do you serve those who are in need? Are you kind to passers-by, the pilgrims on the way who seek your hospitality? Then remember, sure as the sun rises in the East, all these things will return to you, making your life beautiful and bright as a rose garden in the season of spring!

The respect and dignity you accord to another should not depend on *his* status, *his* bank balance or *his* position or the size of *his* car and *his* bungalow or even the colour of *his* skin: rather, it should be determined by *your* dignity and *your* sense of justice as a human being.

There was a time when humanity lost this sense of dignity and justice—and this led to the shameful practice of slavery, genocide and apartheid.

The French writer and thinker Voltaire rues the fact that many men, leaders and rulers are born with a violent tendency for domination, wealth and pleasure; this is made worse by a strong taste for idleness. Consequently, he argues, men covet the money, land and property belonging to other men—and this leads to subjugation and intolerance.

From 1950 to 1990, the world witnessed a protracted period of civil unrest and popular rebellion, when people in several parts of the globe rose together against such prejudice which led to gross inequality and social injustice. This process of moving towards equality under the law was a long and painful process in countries like South Africa. In Northern Ireland, Catholics felt that they were denied equal rights; in Africa, blacks felt unequal under white regimes; even in America, the world's richest and most 'liberal' country, blacks demanded civil rights that were denied to them.

Let us not forget that women too, were subject to severe discrimination and shameful degradation. The issue of women's equality also had to be fought for. While political equality—the right to vote—was accorded to women in the early twentieth century, economic equality was not so easy to achieve. And sad to say, barbaric and inhuman practices like female infanticide are still prevalent in the world's largest democracy!

In India, Mahatma Gandhi was a seasoned crusader for women's equality. Under his leadership, women emerged from restriction to play leading roles in India's independence struggle. Gandhi never considered women to be unfit for any position or task. "To call women sex symbols is a libel," he wrote. "It is man's injustice to women." He also campaigned for women to become equal participants in family and social life. "The wife is not the husband's slave, but his companion, his helpmate and his equal partner in all his joys and sorrows," he asserted. "She is as free as the husband to choose her own path."

When I talk about Gandhi's respect for women, how could I fail to mention the quiet revolution brought about by my Master and mentor, Sadhu Vaswani? In the days before the term "women's rights" was even coined, Gurudev Sadhu Vaswani offered the *purdah-clad*, kitchen-bound women of Sind, *spiritual liberation* in the true sense of the term. His *Sakhi Satsang* (spiritual fellowship of sisters) enabled many women to become decision-makers for the first time in their personal lives—by the very act of voluntarily joining his *satsang*. It would be no exaggeration to say that he inducted Sindhi women into what had, until then, been the domain of men—the practice of religion in the truest sense.

He did everything he could do to break the shackles of superstition and hidebound 'customs' that had kept Sindhi women restricted and confined for centuries. He spoke out against the *purdah* and the evil system of dowry.

His *Sakhi Satsang* was quite revolutionary in its spiritual, moral, social, cultural and economic impact on Sindhi women, if one were to consider the movement in all its aspects. Above all, he emphasised the spiritual *shakti* of women, exclaiming aloud to the male-dominated society, "The woman soul will lead us, upward, on!"

In its Declaration on the Principles of Tolerance, UNESCO offers a definition of tolerance which I find beautiful:

> Tolerance is respect, acceptance and appreciation of the rich diversity of our world's cultures, our forms of expression and ways of being human. Tolerance is harmony in difference.

May I quote here, the words of Rabbi Menachem Mendel:

> Intolerance lies at the core of evil. Not the intolerance that results from any threat or danger. But intolerance of another being who dares to exist. Intolerance

without cause. It is so deep within us, because every human being secretly desires the entire universe to himself. Our only way out is to learn compassion without cause. To care for each other simply because that 'other' exists.

Harmony in difference! This is what the world needs today. We need to think, feel and act in such a way, that we contribute to our own sense of inner peace, and also pave the way of peace among people and nations. For this, we need to respect all those who are unlike us.

Live and let live! This is tolerance at its best. Why should I force my neighbour to think and work and speak and worship as I do? Let me accept that all of us are different—and let me respect the difference. For all our differences, for all our diversity in language, culture and religion, we share but one world. Therefore, let us accept differences—nay, celebrate all differences, and take delight in them! In difference is variety, the spice of life. In diversity is strength.

In India, we celebrate the plurality and multiplicity of our languages and cultures. The poet Subramanya Bharati described Mother India as the glorious lady who spoke eighteen different languages and had thirty million different faces to show. My friends, that was nearly a hundred years ago. Our population was then just thirty million, and the British recognised only eighteen Indian languages. Today, we are a nation of a billion people, and experts say our people speak over two hundred dialects!

You might turn round to point out to me that today, India faces strife and deadly feuds in the name of religion. But I believe that religion came to unite, to reconcile, to create harmony among us. If we quarrel in the name of religion, let us not blame religion for our aberrations: it is not religion which has failed us. It is we who have failed religion!

I always say that people who hurt and kill in the name of religion, are killing their own brethren: for the surest way to reincarnate in a particular race or religion, is to hate that particular religion. It has truly been said that religious hatred and intolerance will become like the express train that will carry you into the religion you hate!

Prejudice, insensitivity and bigotry can poison the best cultures, if we are not careful. Therefore, we must practice, tolerance—the sterling virtue that teaches us to respect people who are different from us.

When patriotism becomes fanatical and narrow, it leads to hatred across borders. When nationalism becomes closed and restrictive, it degenerates into aggression and hegemony. In a world that talks of superpowers and domination, let me say to you: what we need for lasting peace is mutual respect among people, mutual respect between nations.

Respect others—therefore, do not judge others harshly. The trouble with most of us, as Leo Tolstoy points out, is that everyone wants to change humanity while nobody thinks of changing himself! And if one cannot change one's own thinking, how can one change reality?

Mrs. Vijayalakshmi Pandit tells us of the time when she was head of the Indian Delegation to the United Nations, and had to handle India's complaint regarding the treatment of the people of Indian origin in the then apartheid regime of South Africa. Harsh words were used by both sides. The White South African officials used derogatory language to make personal attacks against India's integrity—and also against Mrs. Pandit.

Extremely agitated, Mrs. Pandit at first retaliated with the same sharp weapons. One day, after a particularly nasty and heated duel of words, she was suddenly reminded of Mahatma Gandhi whom she had known, loved and revered all her life.

Would Gandhi approve of what we are doing, she asked herself. In all his hard-fought struggles against the British Empire, never ever had Gandhi offered hatred or disrespect to the colonizers. The best among the British colonial authorities had also respected the Mahatma. Their fight was purely on principles.

Mrs. Pandit did not want to win the debate through questionable tactics, personal attacks and a vindictive spirit that would ruin her own self-respect. Deliberately, consciously, she made a decision to *raise* the level of the debate—to lift it to the plane of diplomacy where it belonged. Let the White South Africans attack her personally; she would not hit out at them to score a cheap point. Though her opponents at first continued their hate campaign, they were forced to abandon their aggressive tactics and rise to the new high level that she had set for the debate.

Weeks later, when the debate was finally over, Mrs. Pandit crossed the floor to meet the leader of the opposing delegation. She held out her hand to him and said, simply, "I have come to ask you to forgive me if I have hurt you by any word or action in this debate."

Needless to say, her gesture was much appreciated! Our own self-respect must lead us on to respect others. As Mrs. Pandit observes, "It is good to feel right with others, but even *better* to feel right with oneself."

The notorious 'apartheid' regime of South Africa denied racial equality to blacks and 'coloured' people. The word apartheid, literally meaning 'apartness' in the Afrikaans language, was a terrible system of racial segregation that was enforced in the Republic of South Africa from 1948 to 1984. Even before 1948, South Africa, which had long been ruled by whites, was racist in its policies and practices. Apartheid was designed to give legal sanction for continued economic and political dominance by people of European descent, while denying basic rights to native South Africans.

Under apartheid, people were legally classified according to their racial groups—white, black or coloured—i.e. of mixed descent. They were geographically and forcibly separated from each other. The black majority were herded into 'homelands' not of their choice. Black people were offered inferior education, medical care and other public services. A separate Amenities Act actually created segregated beaches, buses, hospitals, schools and universities. Blacks were not even part of the common voters' roll—they had a separate voters' roll. Racial discrimination in work and employment was legalised. If a black man was employed in a city and had the 'pass' to live there, his wife and children were denied the right to live with him! They were confined to non-white areas. These black townships often had no plumbing or electricity. Blacks had to travel in separate buses, which had separate stops. On trains, they were not allowed to travel by first or second class.

The apartheid regime was condemned internationally as racist and unjust. Apartheid was declared as a crime against humanity.

After peaceful protests failed to have any effect, black Africans took to armed resistance and acts of sabotage, and South Africa passed through troubled times. Brutal police and military action became the order of the day.

I would like to draw your attention to one fact: as the majority of blacks were excluded from service in the army and police, all white males had to be conscripted for national service. Unwilling to fight racist battles, many white males actually fled from South Africa.

Internal violence, international condemnation and changing demographic conditions finally brought about the winds of change. Reforms were gradually introduced—and a five year state of emergency lasted from 1985 to1990. On February 11, 1990, Nelson Mandela, the black African leader walked out of prison, after 27 years of incarceration.

The legal apartments of apartheid were abolished, but massacres continued across the country, even as a new constitution was being negotiated. On April 27, 1994, freedom finally came to South Africa's blacks.

In 1993, Nelson Mandela and F.W. de Clerk were awarded the Nobel Prize for Peace for bringing to an end the hated apartheid regime.

The lessons of apartheid must always serve as a warning to mankind-that inequalities and discrimination perpetrated by force will only work towards the detriment of all people! South Africa is still struggling to remove economic inequality and empower its black people.

We in India, cannot talk of apartheid in South Africa without recalling Mahatma Gandhi's memorable role in the early days of this cruel system. Of course, apartheid had not been institutionalised at that time, but the evil spirit of intolerance, racial prejudice and inequality had been rampant in South Africa, ever since the Boer occupation.

When Gandhi arrived in Durban, South Africa, in 1893, to serve as legal counsel to the merchant Dada Abdulla, he was asked to undertake a trip to Pretoria. This journey took Gandhi to Pietermaritzburg—an unknown railway station. Gandhi purchased a first-class ticket and took his seat in the first-class compartment. He did not realise that as a non-white, he was not allowed to travel in first class.

Very soon, the railway officials ordered Gandhi to move to the van compartment, where 'coolies' and non-whites were supposed to take their seats. When Gandhi protested that he had purchased a first-class ticket, he was forcibly removed from the train, and his luggage was tossed out on to the platform.

"It was winter," Gandhi wrote in his autobiography, "And the cold was extremely bitter. My overcoat was in my luggage, but I did not dare to ask for it lest I should be insulted again, so I sat and shivered."

This event prompted Gandhi to take a stand against "the deep disease of colour prejudice". In South Africa—and subsequently, in India—as history recalls.

In a just end to the tale of Gandhi's humiliation at Pietermaritzburg Railway Station, in 1997, Nelson Mandela, the President of South Africa, righted a century—old wrong when he conferred the Freedom of Pietermaritzburg on Mahatma Gandhi. President Mandela also recalled "Gandhi's magnificent example of personal sacrifice and dedication in the face of oppression."

If you visit Pietermaritzburg today, you will be delighted to see a bronze statue of Gandhi which stands in Church Street, in the city center!

Today, the word *apartheid*, thankfully, is politically defunct. The apartheid regime has been rejected by the world community at large, and also by native South Africans, and the transition to a democratic republic, with power devolving to the black majority, has been achieved in a remarkably smooth manner.

If I am talking about the horrors of apartheid now, it is only to remind ourselves that we must not let intolerance, prejudice and hatred ever enter our personal, social or professional lives.

Rascism, casteism, and all related practices must be condemned for the evils they perpetrate—discrimination against people founded on false notions of superiority and inferiority; discrimination on the grounds of descent, ethnicity, color or physical characteristics; violent expressions of hostility, hate and bias; perpetuation of social injustice and inequality leading to intergenerational inequality.

Victor Frankel was a survivior of a Nazi concentration camp. Here is what he says in his memoirs:

We who lived in the concentration camps can remember those who walked through the huts comforting others, giving away their last piece of bread . . . They may have been few in number, but they offer sufficient proof that everything can be taken from us but the last of human freedoms . . . the freedom to choose our spirit in any circumstance.

It was a wise thinker who pointed out that there are two great sources of power, two great forces of strength in this world: one of them is vested in those who hate: those who are not afraid to kill, hurt, wound, maim and destroy. The other is vested in those who are not afraid to love, forgive, heal and be reconciled.

Yes, we must be unafraid to love—for it requires courage. I have always believed that the power of love is far greater than the power of hatred. If we are to confront the dark forces of destruction and annihilation, we must use the greatest weapon in our possession—the power of love.

Love is not weak. Love is not sentimental. And love is not always easy!

Once, Mother Teresa was being interviewed for BBC Television. The interviewer remarked that in a way, the life of service might be much easier for her than for ordinary householders. After all, he pointed out, she had no possessions, no insurance, no car and no husband to care for!

Mother Teresa smiled and said to him, "I'm married too!" She held up the ring that nuns of the Order of the Sisters of Charity wear, to symbolise their "marriage" to Christ. She added, "He can be very difficult at times!"

It takes courage to love!

Equally, it takes courage to forgive. Gandhiji urged us to meet the tragedies of life with what he called "soul force". True it is that forgiveness is not weak or naive. It requires courage and clarity.

Love is a mighty force indeed! And so it has been said: there is no hardship, no difficulty that love cannot conquer; no distance that love cannot span; no barrier that love cannot overcome.

I have always said that hate cannot be conquered by hate; so too discrimination can only be wiped out if each one of us fosters tolerance, love and understanding at home and at the work place.

Here is a declaration that a friend sent to me from Tolerance.org, an award-winning website that promotes tolerance, equality and non-discrimination. It is a pledge that each of us must take:

I, (Your Name) will:

- *Examine my own biases and work to overcome them.*
- *Set a positive example of non-discriminatory practices for my family and friends.*
- *Work for equality and understanding in my own community.*
- *Speak out against hate, injustice and all forms of discrimination.*

How can we overcome the negative traits of intolerance, prejudice and hatred? So let me offer you a few practical suggestions:

1. Learn to forgive and forget all injuries and insults dealt to you:

   Revenge and retaliation are best left to time. Let us, in the words of the Lord's prayer, 'forgive those who trespass against us.' The impulse to take revenge only leads to negative *karma.* As Mahatma Gandhi observed, "The law of an eye for an eye makes the whole world blind."

2. Learn to be responsible for your thoughts, words and actions:

We must accept the responsibility for all that happens to us. We always practise this perfectly, when good things happen to us. If I stand first in an examination, I am happy to take all the credit. If my business prospers, I attribute it to my hardwork and sagacity. But what if I am faced with troubles and difficulties?

What, when the going is rough?

If we continue to 'pass the buck', blame others for our failures and troubles, we only accumulate intolerance and prejudice. Instead, we must learn to accept the responsibility for our own destiny, and sow the seeds of good *karma*.

3. Refrain from causing pain to others:

When we harm others, we are paving the way for harming ourselves in the future! We will do well to pause before we act in anger, and reflect upon the consequences of our action.

4. Seek guidance from your Guru, or a spiritual elder:

Most of us lack the mental and spiritual strength to wage the battle of life alone. But the wonderful thing is: we are not alone! Divine guidance, divine grace is always available to those who seek it. Turn to your Guru or to a spiritual teacher who will help you overcome negative *karmic* patterns.

5. Work towards your own liberation:

Many of us are apt to imagine that liberation from our own deeply felt prejudice and hatred is not attainable for the likes of us. This is a defeatist, pessimistic attitude. When we set our sights firmly on the goal of inner peace and harmony, we accelerate the pace of our own spiritual evolution. This is achieved through *bhakti* (devotion), *seva* (service) and *sadhana* (practice of austerities like meditation). By consciously setting out to purify ourselves thus, we can conquer the negativities that poison us from the inside and destroy us from within, like a cancer of the spirit.

6. Refuse to degrade yourself by hatred:

   Hatred is a destructive and corrosive emotion. It demeans you; it hurts those whom you hate. Do not allow your spirit to be poisoned by hatred. You deserve more respect from yourself!

Subject yourself to periodical self-examination: do you harbour hatred towards any individual/any group of people? If the answer is yes, ask yourself how comfortable you are being filled with something as ugly and poisonous as hatred.

Hatred is a disease. Love is the cure. Even if someone does something you don't agree with or understand, you should love them. Hating will destroy you long before it does them.

—**Anonymous**

Mullah Nasruddin's Judgement

Mullah Nasruddin was once chosen as a honorary magistrate. As he was listening to the first case, he decided that he would impress everyone by delivering an impeccable verdict. As soon as one side of the case had been presented, he rose and announced to the court that he would deliver the verdict within five minutes.

The court clerk was dismayed. He hastily whispered to the Mullah, "How can you do that? You haven't listened to the other side yet!" Mullah shot back, "Now, don't confuse me. I am now clear with the verdict that I am about to declare. If I listen to the other side, I am bound to get confused!"

This is how a prejudiced mind functions. It can only see one side of the picture and is firm in its conviction that it sees the whole truth.

PRACTICAL TIP:

Analyse your hatred logically. Try to examine the reason why your hatred exists. Is it because of fear, or jealousy, or because of the effect that someone or something has on you or your life? Once you do this (list your reasons or write them down on paper) you will often find that there are no real reasons why you hate something or someone so much. At most it is a minor annoyance which can easily be overcome.

6

Inferiority Complex

The term 'complex' in psycho analysis refers to a combination of emotions and impulses that have been rejected from awareness, but still influence a person's behavior. It is a state of thinking, an attitude with which we have not really come to terms; the tendency of the complex is to draw unrelated ideas into itself. The word has now come to mean simply, "An exaggerated or obsessive concern or fear".

Most of us understand inferiority complex to be an intense feeling of inferiority, resulting in a personality characterised either by extreme reticence or, as a result of overcompensation, by extreme aggressiveness. In common parlance, it refers to lack of self-esteem; feeling of inadequacy; lack of self-confidence and low self-worth.

All of us go through feelings of inferiority occasionally. Many students, for instance, feel a sense of inadequacy and fear when they see others start writing fast and furiously at the start of the examination. Competitors in a race feel stressed when they see rivals rushing past them. Debators awaiting their turn at the podium, become nervous and insecure when they hear their competitors holding forth eloquently to the cheers and applause of the audience. Such a feeling is normal and can often act as an incentive for higher achievements. But a complex is something far more deep seated; it is deeply rooted in the subconscious, causing the individual to overcompensate through aggression or retreat.

What are the causes of inferiority complex? Psychologists talk of four broad reasons:

1. Parental Attitudes: Children who are brought up in authoritarian families and are subjected to constant fault-finding and criticism often grow up with an inferiority complex. Many of them grow up in the belief that they are 'inadequate, incompetent and inferior' to quote an expert.

2. Physical Defects: Any physical deformity or even non-critical defects like a squint or thin legs, abnormal facial features and speech defects give rise to excessive emotional reactions, and become compounded with earlier unpleasant experiences.

3. Mental Limitations: Insecurity and low self-worth are created when unfair comparisons are made with other ('superior') people and their achievements.

4. Social Disadvantages: The background, class, family and status of an individual may also aggravate feelings of inferiority.

Psychological theory cannot account satisfactorily for all aspects of human nature and human behaviour! And thus we have many strong-willed, emotionally balanced people with pronounced physical defects; we have great leaders and entrepreneurs coming from disadvantaged sections of society, who have never let their background hamper them. The reasons cited above are only to be taken as indicative factors, and not the only causes for inferiority complex.

The distinguished psychologist Adler talks about primary and secondary complexes in this connection: a primary inferiority complex arises from a deep-rooted feeling of helplessness in the child's psyche, from his early experiences; whereas a secondary complex is related to his adult experiences of being unable to reach the levels of success that he has set out for himself. Thus the complex arises out of subtle imagination as well as external conditioning.

Dear readers, I am no expert in neurotic theory! I share some of these theories that I have read merely to help laymen like us understand what this painful and debilitating complex is all about; and also to help us treat our children, siblings and friends with understanding and appreciation so that they are not made to go through a sense of such inadequacy and helplessness! We are not all of us trained counsellors that we can recognise symptoms and offer appropriate therapy; but surely we are all capable of becoming understanding, sensitive individuals who care for the welfare of others!

How is the inferiority complex manifested in behaviour? Through two modes: withdrawal or aggression. In the first case, the individual becomes extremely self-conscious and sensitive, and keeps aloof from social contacts. In the second case, as if to overcompensate for his own feeling of inadequacy, the individual becomes aggressive, seeks attention, criticises others or tends to overdo his part. Withdrawal is far more common than aggression, in individuals who are victims of this complex. Other observable attributes include:

- Extreme embarrassment or extreme shyness
- Timidity
- Fear and bewilderment in company of peers and others
- Sensitivity to all forms of criticism
- Resentment of criticism
- Rebellion against corrections/suggestions for improvement
- Desire for praise
- Defense of their own actions
- Aloofness from social contacts
- Day-dreaming/ fantasising

- Pretended illness
- Bitterness towards others
- Constant irritability
- Undue worry

Psychologists add that extreme defense mechanisms may include denial of reality, distortion of reality, retreat from reality, attack on reality and compromise with reality. In other words, reality is denied by repressing a given impulse and denying its existence; however, emotions are difficult to repress, and they often occur later in disguised form.

My only purpose in sharing the above information is to help my readers recognise these symptoms in friends and acquaintances and deal with such issues sensitively. As I said earlier, all of us feel inadequate or inferior on some occasion or the other. We may even recognise some of the above symptoms in ourselves! The point is to become aware of them, deal with them effectively and stop them from becoming impediments to our own inner peace, sense of balance and personal happiness.

> Your time is limited, so don't waste it living someone else's life. Don't be trapped by dogma—which is living with the results of other people's thinking. Don't let the noise of others' opinions drown out your own inner voice. And most important, have the courage to follow your heart and intuition. They somehow already know what you truly want to become. Everything else is secondary.
>
> —Steve Jobs

Let me repeat my *mantra:* happiness is our birthright as children of God! It is our duty to attain to this true happiness by conquering our weaknesses and promoting our true strengths.

How can we help prevent this complex in those we love? Let us first deal with the aspect of prevention in childhood:

1. We should treat our children with love and sensitivity. We should not make them unhappy by constant unfavourable comparisons with their peers.

2. We should not set unreal standards and levels of success for them to achieve.

3. We must offer encouragement and appreciation instead of merely insisting on competition.

4. We must create opportunities of success in the child's area of interest instead of insisting that he should succeed in our area of focus. For instance, we may want the child to stand first in class; but he may want to dance, sing or paint.

5. We can give the child responsibilities at home that he can fulfill and reward him with praise for every job that is well done.

6. We should encourage the child to develop skills that will contribute to his sense of self-worth.

It is said that the child's greatest security lies in the personal feeling of affection and love created by the parents at home. Let me add too, that love for God, prayer and childhood training in spiritual exercises like *kirtan*, yoga and meditation can do wonders for the wholesome development of our children!

As for adults: my view of the solution is simplicity itself. If you or your friends suffer from such a complex, my humble advice to you is: know yourself; accept yourself; believe in yourself; love and respect yourself for your unique attributes; do your best at all times and leave the rest to God!

I am not suggesting that all of us are perfect; each and every one of us has certain inborn negative traits and weaknesses that we must struggle to overcome. But the mature approach is to recognise these weaknesses, identify them and work on them so that they may be successfully eliminated.

Let me give you a small example: stammering was a common speech defect among many children in those days; the therapy practised by many parents was just patience, love and constant training for the child in repetition of its utterances and slowing down of speech. Thus what could become a major embarrassment for the child was successfully averted by simple measures at home. Only when we identify and recognise our weaknesses can we deal with them and overcome them successfully.

People with deep seated neuroses and complexes are often told to 'seek therapy' or go to a psychiatric counsellor. But in India, most people do not see this as a practical option, as we have traditionally relied on our own social and familial support systems. How can we help others—our peers, friends, family members, colleagues and other adults who suffer from a sense of inferiority? In general, I would say this applies to all people you may come across: first and foremost, by putting aside our own sense of superiority and egoism, and recognising the fact that it takes all types of people to make this world what it is! And secondly, by learning to appreciate people for what they are, rather than constantly devaluing them for what they are not.

No one can make you inferior without your consent.

—Eleanor Roosevelt

The following suggestions may also be of help in dealing with people you are close to:

1. Encourage them to talk about themselves, give vent to their suppressed feelings, especially their past hurts, in an environment that is non-judgemental and free from fault-finding.

2. Allow them to express their fears and frustrations and deal with these in a spirit of compassion and understanding.

3. Help them appreciate their own gifts and unique talents.

4. Assure them that they have something valuable to offer to the world.

5. Strong and loyal friendship is the best support that you can give such people. Spending time in the company of a positive friend can be the best way of improving the self-esteem of such people.

6. If at first, the individual refuses to open up to you, you can gift inspirational books or CDs to him, so that he becomes aware that he can help himself.

Choose your role models carefully!

What do you wish to be like? Whom do you like to emulate?

In the '50s or '60s, youngsters often cited Jawaharlal Nehru or Subash Chandra Bose as their role models. These men were perceived as eminent personalities because they had dedicated their lives for a cause they believed in, and contributed to the nation's good.

Today, role models are largely 'famous' people who are in the glare of media light. These are the celebrities most talked about, most publicised and most 'exposed' by the media glare. Chances are, the role models chosen by today's youth will be film stars, cricketers or fashion ikons.

These men and women have obviously worked hard, perhaps struggled hard to reach their position of eminence. Their grit and determination may well be worth emulating. But the fear is that they may be admired or emulated for all the wrong reasons! You can't take on a film star as a role model because he owns a bungalow and a Mercedes Benz! You cannot take on a businessman as a role model because he is a millionaire!

Do you think you might have traces of inferiority complex?

Try to answer the following questions as truthfully as possible:

1. Do you tend to withdraw from social contacts?
2. Do you blame fate/fortune/environment for your problems?
3. Do you refrain from complimenting peers/friends/colleagues for their achievements?
4. Are you sensitive to compliments/criticism from others?
5. Are you often timid/shy or embarrassed in company?
6. Do you tend to compare yourself with others unfavourably? ("She is so tall" or "He is so confident" or "I wish I had her good looks" or "She is much smarter than me").
7. What is your attitude towards people who are better than you in certain areas of your life? How do you feel towards people who are more attractive than you? How do you feel towards people who are your superiors at work? Do you feel inferior to them? Do you feel they are better than you? Do you need to "pull" them down from their podium by criticising? Are you envious or resentful towards them?

If your answer to most of the above questions is "Yes" then you need to develop a greater sense of self-esteem!

Here are a few practical suggestions to build your sense of self-worth:

1. Realise that you are unique—you have been created with certain traits and gifts that are special to you. Because you are not aware of them, it does not mean you are worthless. Try and find out your special strengths and gifts: your friends/teachers/family will only be too happy to point them out for you.

2. Think of what you enjoy doing—singing, dancing, storytelling, drawing, calligraphy, cooking, gardening . . . recreate the sense of pleasure and enjoyment that you derive from these activities, and add more such activities to your daily routine.

3. Participate in the social activities of your group, your community and your neighbourhood. Do not allow yourself to become isolated from your neighbours and friends. Connecting with others, participating in such activities draws you out and gives you the awareness that you are part of a cosmic whole.

4. Give more meaning to your life by finding a worthy cause to which you can devote your energies—it may be an NGO, a *satsang*, a social service group or anything you believe in.

5. Learn to be kind to yourself! Do not criticise yourself or call yourself names constantly! Take good care of yourself physically and mentally.

6. Avoid the company of people who put you down constantly. Do not allow others' criticism to affect your self-image.

7. Make a difference to others—and you will see the difference in your attitude and personal life! Therefore, go out of your way to help others and make life better for them.

8. Above all, always remember that God loves you and created you to fulfill His special purpose. When you know that He loves you and trusts you, how can you think poorly of yourself?

Aimee Mullins runs track events; she also happens to be a double amputee, who uses artificial limbs—or prosthetics as they are called. Once, as she was preparing for a race, she felt that her prosthetics were not comfortable. She went to her coach, a tough old sportsman from Brooklyn and asked to be excused from the race. She was afraid if she continued running her leg might come off in the middle of the race.

"Aimee, so what if your leg falls off?" he scolded her. "You pick it up, you put it back on, and you finish the race."

In her book, *Aimee Mullins on Running*, she tells us that she simply handed over to him her fear—and he responded not with pity, but with humour. And along with that affectionate reprimand, he handed her back courage.

PRACTICAL TIP:

Remember you are unique!

Stop comparing yourself with others. Stop all negative self-talk. ("Nobody likes me." "I am too short." "She is laughing at my clumsiness" Etc.) Instead, try positive visualization. Picture yourself happy, laughing, confident, doing your work well. Be yourself! Don't try to live your life imitating others. Recognise and celebrate your achievements and victories, however small they are.

7
Laziness

━━━━━ ⟡ ━━━━━

Maharishi Patanjali, the author of that world-renowned treatise *Yoga Shastra*, tells us in his remarkable work: "There are several obstacles which are to be expected on the path of the aspirant on his inner journey, which bring with them several consequences that grow out of them."

vyadhi styana samshaya pramada alasya avirati bhranti-darshana alabdha-bhumikatva anavasthitatva chitta vikshepa te antarayah . . .

Nine kinds of distractions are mentioned as obstacles encountered on the path: disease, mental dullness, constant doubt, carelessness, laziness, sensual craving, false perception, failure and instability: these constitute distractions and disturbances on the path of Yoga.

Let me tell you friends: laziness, dullness, sloth, inertia and mental fatigue are not only detrimental to yoga; they are also impediments that do not permit you to live life fully!

"Laziness is not a big deal!" some of my young friends tell me. "We all need to relax, chill, take it easy occasionally. It is no sin to let go every now and then!"

I beg to differ! I agree with Eleanor Roosevelt who said: "So much attention is paid to the aggressive sins, such as violence and cruelty and greed with all their tragic effects, that too little attention is paid to the passive sins, such as apathy and laziness, which in the long run can have a more devastating and destructive effect upon society than the others."

Passive sin, is how she describes laziness, which, incidentally is associated with *tamasic* qualities such as inertia, sloth and dullness. And let me add that laziness is not relaxation; relaxation comes after hard work; laziness precludes and prevents hardwork!

Let me quote from the *Book of Proverbs:*

> How long will you lie there, O sluggard?
> When will you arise from your sleep?
> A little sleep, a little slumber,
> A little folding of the hands to rest,
> And poverty will come upon you like a robber,
> And want like an armed man.

The sluggard is also ticked off ruthlessly:

> Go to the ant, O sluggard;
> Consider her ways, and be wise.
> Without having any chief,
> Officer, or ruler,
> She prepares her bread in summer
> And gathers her food in harvest.

That is surely a sharp whiplash on those of us who work only when we are being watched!

Laziness manifests itself in all sorts of insidious aspects in people's everyday life. For some, it becomes an untimely indulgence, as happened with the tortoise who decided to take a nap at the most inopportune moment in the race; for some, it becomes habitual, like stubborn children who refuse to do their homework; for some of us, it is built into our routine, as it happens with grown men and women who spend hours before the TV watching mindless entertainment programmes; for yet others, it becomes an attitude to work, as they master the art of shirking work and following the path of least effort and least contribution even in their paid employment. Getting away with as little work as possible becomes their motto.

In Physics, inertia is defined as that property of matter by which it remains at rest unless acted upon by some external force; in human nature, inertia (inertness) is an indisposition or unwillingness for movement, exertion or change of any kind. Thus we speak of the inertia of government offices, now referred to as bureaucratic red tape. Even as I write this, the European debt crisis is causing concern in world markets, and experts are blaming the inertia of European leaders for their inability to respond to the situation!

Idleness, indolence, laziness, listlessness, sloth are all shades of inertia; the opposite of these are drive, industriousness, application, the impulse to take charge and get going!

Sloth is an attitude that puts physical comfort and disinclination to strive before all else; it makes people disregard their duties and responsibilities and shows scant respect for others. Christian saints warn us that spiritual sloth is even worse: for it makes us disregard our responsibilities to God and our own souls.

Do you keep your daily appointment with God? Do you remember Him without fail in prayer and devotion? Do you spend a little time everyday reading the scriptures or the *bani* of saints? Do you spare a thought and a little effort to ease the suffering of others? If your answer to all these questions is No, then you are indeed guilty of spiritual sloth!

Experts say that there is something called a "comfort zone" for each one of us: it is nothing but a mental conditioning by which we create our own boundaries which suit us and our sense of comfort and security: we choose to stay within these bounds, and refuse to step out. Without exception, all successful people are known to have boldly stepped out of their comfort zones to accomplish their goals and desires! If we stick to our comfort zones, we would never learn new skills and achieve better performance. Inertia and mental indolence stops us from doing this. We are content with the status quo; we lack drive and ambition; we are content to let things drift . . .

Such an attitude is stifling, constricting for us and others. We perform well below our potential. Our God-given talents and abilities lie unused and dormant. We get into a mental and physical rut, and allow this inertia to dictate to us what we can do and cannot do. The saddest part is that we have created this rut ourselves, and we have to rouse ourselves physically and mentally, if we are to get out of it and get on with life. If we don't make this effort to free ourselves—we are sentencing ourselves to a life of underperformance and failure.

I think the many 'diversions' and so-called 'pastimes' now available to us are largely responsible for the increase in sloth and indolence today: no matter what is happening, we do not want to miss our favourite TV programmes; never mind if we are needed at work, we take days off to watch cricket matches; no matter what our work responsibilities are, we have to 'go' on Facebook or check our email frantically every 15 minutes . . . no wonder that these shallow activities are called 'diversion'; they divert us from the important task of purposeful living!

What is your diversion? Watching football or cricket matches? Browsing the internet? Watching an endless stream of movies? Or just curling up on the sofa with junk food and high-fat snacks?

An amusing article I read a few years back describes all modern 'gadgets' as sloth-inducing! In the good old days, when we wanted to know something or find out something important, we would go to the library and spend a lot of time looking up the appropriate reference books, reading, summarising, making notes. Now, we don't even want to go to a computer: we prefer to lie on the sofa with that ultimate gadget of the couch potato, the palm-held I-pad! They tell me we now have auto-geared cars with cruise control which don't even require you to press your feet on the clutch pedals. "In other words," the writer concludes, "for some time now, progress has moved beyond preserving human dignity to encouraging human sloth. Far from being a sin, it has become an aspiration." The writer adds interestingly, that the Catholic Church began to use the term sloth in its list of deadly sins, instead of the original term 'sadness' (Greek: *acedia*, or not caring) around the time of the Industrial Revolution! It has now led us into an exit-less cul-de-sac: "Sloth is bad because it impedes progress; progress is good because it enables us to be slothful."

As we saw earlier, Christian morality regards sloth as a deadly sin. St. Thomas Aquinas defined sloth as "sluggishness of the mind which neglects to begin good."

Many western writers tell us that Satan will always find 'business' for idle hands and idle minds. In the words of the saying all of us know, "an idle mind is the devil's workshop."

Many people regard meditation and contemplation as 'lazy' or 'slothful'. Nothing could be further from the truth. Buddhism describes indolence and torpor as *thina-middha*, one of the hindrances to the perception of truth. Those of you who have practised meditation can surely vouch for this: that meditation is not idleness; it is spiritually alert and energising, and it improves concentration and focus, actually helping us to overcome sloth. As for those of you who fall asleep during Meditation, well, you have not been meditating at all! Recently, a group of psychologists in Australia actually proclaimed that laziness is now taking on the characteristics of a mental disease, which they have labelled motivational deficiency disorder or MoDeD! Responding to their research paper which was published in the prestigious *BMJ* or *British Medical Journal*, a 'victim' of the disease retorted that the disease brought its own economic benefits: "MoDeD sufferers are responsible for an estimated 35% of consumption of snack foods, 40% of viewing of all reality TV shows, and 45% of all purchases of popular music. In addition, MoDeD sufferers produce 35% fewer greenhouse gases because of their tendencies to stay at home. A more comprehensive analysis of the full economic impact of MoDeD should be done, preferably by someone other than me."

The *Dhammapada* uses the example of a lazy animal to warn against sloth. "When torpid and over-fed, a sleepy-head lolling about like a stout hog, fattened on fodder: a dullard enters the womb over and over again (23:325)."

Thus, according to Buddhist thought, a slothful life results in rebirth and the perpetuation of the cycle of *karma*.

I would not go so far! But I must admit that laziness is linked to several serious problems like procrastination, apathy, inertia, obesity, depression and what we can only call couch potato-syndrome or addiction to the sofa and the idiot box.

The Tirukkural has a whole chapter which warns us against sloth and laziness: In Chapter 61, entitled Idleness, the saint-poet Thiruvalluvar tells us:

1. The Family is an ever-lit lamp, which loses its bright light when it is clouded by the pollution of idleness.

2. If you wish to make your home radiant, avoid idleness.

3. If you express your mental lethargy in your conduct, your family will be destroyed before you are!

4. He who indulges in idleness and avoids true effort will grow in weakness and dissipation.

5. Procrastination, forgetfulness, laziness and sleep— these four form the chosen vessel which transports men to their ruin.

6. Even if they acquire the fellowship of emperors who rule the earth, idle men will never prosper.

7. The lazy ones, who are incapable of noble exertion, invite sharp abuses and must endure the shame of scornful words.

8. Idleness will eventually reduce you to becoming a slave of your adversaries.

9. He whose leadership is threatened can overcome his adversity by conquering his idleness.

10. The ruler who is without sloth will achieve all that the good Lord can give him.

While addicts argue whether laziness is a disease or a state of mind, I prefer to take the old fashioned view that laziness is just a disinclination to work.

I am not talking of the Sunday morning mood or the well-earned relaxation during a vacation: I am talking of the refusal to function, the inability to get up and do what has to be done; when we get into a rut and cannot get on with life and its activities; when we sink into a lethargy and don't want to go on . . .

I don't think anyone is born lazy: rather, laziness is a bad habit or a negative trait we acquire due to our own lack of motivation.

Strangely enough, the causes and the effects of laziness are mixed up, making it almost impossible to identify which is which: procrastination, making excuses, refusing to accept your responsibilities. You know what I mean when you consider this: you procrastinate because you are lazy; you are lazy because you procrastinate. You make excuses because you are lazy; you are lazy because you are always making excuses; so it is that you refuse to accept your responsibilities!

But let me warn you: laziness is not to be dismissed as a comical excess; it is a serious issue which can mar your prospects and take you to the brink of failure. It is a dangerous form of escapism, an addictive behaviour pattern that leaves you in lethargy!

Experts say that one or all of the following can lead to a state of chronic inertia or laziness:

1. Lack of alignment between your goals, your values and your abilities
2. Fear of failure
3. Frustration in your work or personal life
4. Lack of purpose
5. Low self-esteem/ lack of self-confidence
6. Creation of a 'comfort zone' which traps you and refuses to let you move ahead
7. "Conditioning" or habit forming lifestyle that promotes laziness
8. Low energy levels—poor health

Let me warn you that none of these can be excuses for indolence and sloth! Each of these factors must be tackled and conquered if you are not to sink into the mire of apathy and lethargy.

> Indolence is a delightful but distressing state; we must be doing something to be happy.
>
> —Mahatma Gandhi

Here are some of the most deadly effects of laziness:

1. Lack of interest and motivation
2. Underachievement/ underperformance

3. Loss of good name
4. Loss of opportunity for advancement
5. Inability to achieve goals and targets
6. Waste of potential and skills
7. Loss of control/loss of direction in life
8. Dependence on others/parasite syndrome
9. Demoralisation
10. Ruin of family life, happiness and prosperity

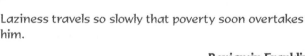

Laziness travels so slowly that poverty soon overtakes him.

—Benjamin Franklin

It is obvious from the above that we must make the effort to break free of laziness. There is a Polish proverb that tells us: *He that wishes to eat the nut must make the effort to crack the shell.* You cannot get what you want without effort. You can't always choose the path of least effort and least resistance; you can't always live for indulgence and pleasure; you cannot live in the present all the time; you have to get started; you have got to move!

Many people are apt to imagine that entrepreneurs, wealthy businessmen and corporate bigwigs are always enjoying a life of pleasure and extravagance; they are far from right. Most of the wealthy men I know are hardworking; they put in longer working hours than many of their employees; they often sacrifice personal time and personal pleasures; they pursue their goal with single-minded determination and focus.

If you are habitually lazy, you can't become a successful businessman overnight. But as a first step towards success, you must break out of the rut of sloth and apathy. Let me also warn young parents who are reading this book: do not spoil your children! Do not indulge them in needless pampering and luxury. Teach them the value of hard work and personal effort when they are young!

As our purpose is, so will our spiritual progress be, and we need to be truly diligent if we wish to progress far. For if a man of firm resolution often encounters failure, how can any who seldom makes any firm resolve achieve anything? We fail in our purposes in various ways, and the omission of our spiritual exercises seldom passes without certain loss to our souls. The resolution of good men depends more on the grace of God than on their own wisdom, and they put their whole trust in Him in all their undertakings . . .

If any of our proper exercises are omitted in order to perform some act of mercy or help a brother, they may be resumed later. But if they are lightly set aside out of sloth or carelessness, this is blameworthy indeed, and will prove harmful to our souls. Try as we will, we shall still fail all too easily in many things. Nevertheless, we should always have a firm resolve, especially against such faults as most hinder our progress. We should carefully examine and order both our inner and outer life, since both are vital to our advance.

—Thomas a Kempis

How can you overcome laziness? So let me offer you a few practical suggestions:

1. Introspect on the reasons for your laziness. What is it that makes you lethargic? Is it that you don't like what you are doing? Consider switching to jobs or courses that offer you greater motivation.

2. Make sure that you are in good health and that illness or disease is not the cause of your lethargy.

3. Seek your own motivation by identifying your goals, and working towards them.

4. Learn the fine art of self-discipline: eat less, sleep less, talk less and spend less time on mindless pleasures and passive forms of entertainment.

5. If you are overwhelmed by the tasks before you, learn to break them up into manageable units and attend to one detail at a time.

6. Break the pattern of sloth and inertia by setting yourself a healthy routine including physical exercise, social contact and completion of long overdue tasks.

7. Adopt a healthy diet. Doctors recommend complex carbohydrates, whole grains, fruits and vegetables and avoidance of alcohol and stimulants.

8. Try energising routines such as *pranayama*, reiki or meditation to improve concentration and overcome negative energy.

9. Adopt a regular exercise routine. Walking is the emperor of all exercises!

10. If, for any reason, you are demotivated, demoralised by your work, and disinclined to carry on with your present employment, consider switching jobs. Do not just quit, but plan your exit strategy. Quitting outright is tough; but it is not dishonourable if you feel your life is being drained away.

PRACTICAL TIP:

Fix a goal and keep an unwavering focus on it all the time. Work towards your goal. Cultivate the determination to achieve it against all odds. Be on your toes—physically and mentally. Never, never, never give up your efforts to achieve what you aspire to!

8

The Failings of Excessive Desire: Lust, Greed and Gluttony

Some of the readers of this book may wonder why I have chosen to deal with these three negative traits under one head: I regard them as failings of the flesh, that arise due to excessive desire or *moha*, as it is referred to in Sanskrit.

Significant are the words of the great lawgiver, Manu: "Desire is never satisfied by the enjoyment of the objects of desire. It grows from more to more, as does the fire to which fuel is added."

The *Yoga Vashishta* too tells us: "We think it is we who enjoy pleasure. But, in truth, it is pleasures which enjoy us. For, while pleasure always remains young and vital, it is we who keep growing old and get consumed in the fire of pleasure."

Kama, lobha, pratyahara—these are three of the most demeaning and degrading negative traits that drag us down to the unregenerate state of the animal within us. They are shameful, humiliating weaknesses that make us slaves to animal appetites and passions. They are *kleshas* or afflictions of the mind. "These *kleshas* are imprinted on *chitta*, the individual consciousness, from time immemorial and create and perpetuate the illusions that our entire human existence is limited to the mind-body complex. Even after death the *chitta* retains the *kleshas* in seed form and they sprout to full fruition in the next incarnation . . ." So Sage Patanjali warns us.

For many of us our so-called consciousness is limited to the bodily existence; we cannot rise beyond the level of the senses and the flesh; thus we are always subject to temptations, always at the mercy of forces beyond our control, desperate to snatch at 'pleasures' which offer gratification of the senses and the passions.

Have you ever seen a fly sipping honey? At first it takes great care to ensure that its legs are free. It sits on the edge of the pot of honey and seems determined to fly away after just one sip. But once it begins to relish the honey, it throws wisdom and caution to the winds. By the time it reaches satiety, it realises that its legs are stuck in honey; there is no escape; it cannot fly away; it is doomed to death in its sweet grave!

So is it with man! He is lured into temptation by the thought of a 'little' pleasure; he is drawn to it *again and again*, until he becomes a slave of the craving which he cannot relinquish; *kama*, desire, lust, he realises too late, is a craving that can never be quenched!

And the temptations that lure man are very many! There is the temptation to gratify the tongue; to drink, to smoke, to indulge in substance abuse; to overeat or eat forbidden food; to amass wealth by fair means or foul . . . the list is endless.

Desire, *trishna* or *moha*, is that well, that deep well into which when a man falls, he is unable to come out. We all stand at the very edge of that well. You may be of high birth, you may have read the scriptures, you may have all the knowledge that books can give. But, once you fall a prey to desire, once you are gripped by the craving to possess something, to indulge your craving, to satiate your passion, you cannot give up, you are unable to relent!

Keep away from desires! It is easier said than done. How can we do this? We must of course heed the Buddha's warning that desire is the root cause of all sorrow. If we really want to be free of misery, sorrow, delusion and disappointment, then we must learn to conquer desires.

There are three types of desires—1) Desire for pleasures of the flesh or lust; 2) Desire for wealth or greed; 3) Desire for power or pride.

Kama or Lust:

Kama is actually one of the *purusharthas*—the third of the four goals of human life according to Hindu philosophy (the other three being *dharma, artha* and *mokasha*). True self-realisation is possible by attaining and balancing these four goals. Perhaps each individual passes through stages of evolution during which each of these goals is sought. Thus, as we grow older and wiser, we overcome the desire to amass more and more wealth, or to seek after material pleasures. Our consciousness turns to the pursuit of the ultimate objective, *Moksha* or Liberation.

How is it that one of the *purusharthas* sanctioned by the scriptures is designated as a *klesha,* or a deadly sin? The answer lies in the degree or the extent to which we pursue it: the key word here is the one I have used in the title of this chapter: excessive. Even *kama* is legitimate within the prescribed limits: it is when we exceed the limits that the pleasure turns to poison. In other words, unrestricted gratification defeats the purpose of true pleasure; *kama* cannot be allowed to dominate our life; it is an impulse which has to be restricted and disciplined. Unrestrained indulgence in *kama* is condemned by all faiths and scriptures as a destructive and evil force.

It is with good reason therefore, that Lust is capitalised and included in the list of Mortal Sins by the Church: the church teaches us that when someone chooses mortal sin they exercise their free will to turn away from God, forfeit heaven and choose hell. That is how severe the transgression is!

One of the greatest works of Medieval literature, Dante's Divine Comedy touches boldly on the sin of lust. Dante's criterion for lust was an "excessive Love of others", insofar as an excessive love for man would render one's love of God secondary.

In the first section of Dante's Inferno, the lustful are punished by being continuously swept around in a whirlwind, which symbolises their passions. The damned lovers who have been guilty of lust, like the famous pair of Paolo and Francesca, receive what they desired in their mortal lives; but their passions enslave them without rest or reprieve for all eternity. In Purgatorio, spirits who are penitent and wish to make amends for their sins of lust, choose to walk through flames in order to purge themselves of their lustful inclinations.

"Many are the keys to good health," Mahatma Gandhi tells us. "No doubt they are all essential; but the one thing needful, above all others, is *brahmacharya.*"

Gurudev Sadhu Vaswani taught us that in ancient India the two great ideals of purity and prayer were brought together in the one great concept of *brahmacharya.* Do not think that *brahmacharya* is limited to just celibacy. *Brahmacharya* can also be practised in married life. *Brahmacharya* is not asceticisim; nor is it stoicism. *Brahamcharya* is literally, moving with God! To move and live in *Brahman*—that is to be a true *brahmachari.* He must be a man of purity and prayer. Purity and prayer make the body and spirit vital. They rejuvenate the outer body, breaking the barriers of weakness. They link man with God: and he finds a great *shakti* (energy) flowing through him. He becomes a channel for the outpouring upon others of the spirit of Light!

Brahmacharya is freedom from lust and carnality. In other words, it is freedom from the coils of the serpent, which is lust.

All the major religions of the world talk about the necessity of self-discipline, especially the control of the lower passions. However, Hindu scriptures have attached a profound significance to the concept of *brahmacharya.* As we saw earlier,

Gurudev Sadhu Vaswani defined *brahmacharya* in a beautiful way—walking with God. Literally, the term also means living and moving with *Brahman*—the Absolute, Divine Self. In its highest form, it implies consciousness of the concept—*Aham Brahmasmi*—"I am Brahman." Thus it relates to the effort to realise our divine potential.

In a specific sense, *brahmacharya* implies the practise of celibacy and restraint of sex indulgences. Thus in ancient India, young disciples and students learning at the feet of a guru in an *ashrama*, were enjoined not to indulge in sensual pleasures and to observe strict celibacy, until they were old enough and mature enough to enter the next stage of life—the *grihastha ashrama* or married life.

Although celibacy and restraint are undoubtedly important aspects of *brahmacharya*, in a broader sense it implies conquest over passions—and the sublimation of the merely biological instinct leading to a profound perception of the self in relation to the Universe.

In its broadest sense, *brahmacharya* denotes purity of character, purity of thought, word and deed. It denotes mastery over the mind and senses, especially over the sexual force. For when the latter is brought under control, all other aspects of our life are automatically brought under control. Such a state of self-discipline is conducive to our health, happiness and spiritual progress. Indeed, *brahmacharya* is a virtue that will help us to lead an active and healthy life for a long period of time.

I am aware that people will find it strange that I talk about *brahmacharya*, which is associated especially with the practice of celibacy, in an age when sexual promiscuity has become rampant. I would only like to remind you that it was "free sex" of this sort that destroyed the ancient civilisations of Babylon, Greece and Rome.

Self-discipline and self-control are the antidotes to lust: and lust is not to be confused with the higher emotion of love! Lust is physical passion and sensation; love is of the mind, heart and spirit; it transcends the physical body and its passions; love is commitment, sacrifice and discipline; lust is wayward, self-seeking and self-gratification. Love makes you better, nobler, wiser; lust only makes you passionate, selfish and jealous. Love can help you move Godward; lust only drags you into depravity. Love is pure and liberating; lust is negative and destructive.

> In lust there is reliance upon the object of sense and consequent spiritual subordination of the soul to it, but love puts the soul into direct and co-ordinate relation with the reality which is behind the form. Therefore lust is experienced as being heavy and love is experienced as being light. In lust there is a narrowing down of life and in love there is an expansion in being . . . If you love the whole world you vicariously live in the whole world, but in lust there is an ebbing down of life and a general sense of hopeless dependence upon a form which is regarded as another. Thus, in lust there is the accentuation of separateness and suffering, but in love there is the feeling of unity and joy . . .
>
> —Avatar Meher Baba

Brahmacharya, as I have said, goes beyond the concept of celibacy, and it includes purification and awakening of consciousness. Such a state of consciousness surely cannot tolerate moral aberrations like the legalisation of abortion and immoral relationships outside marriage.

What we need under the circumstances, is a change of mind, a change of attitude, a transformation of the heart. Suppression or repression will harm us—while transformation of the mind will be a positive effort. And we would also do well to remember that an idle mind is the devil's workshop. An active, useful life with meditation and *naam-japa* in leisure hours will help us lead a well-balanced life.

The mind must be controlled and disciplined to promote mental well-being. Purity of mind is one of the greatest blessings a man or woman can achieve. Regularity, punctuality, clean habits, *sattvic* food and yoga exercises are all beneficial in the practice of *brahmacharya*.

In Chapter 3 of the Gita, the Lord warns us against the deadly effects of *kama*, which He describes as an insatiable fire. Entering through the open gates of the senses, it captures the fortress of the mind and overwhelms our determination and will-power. "Therefore, O Arjuna, control thy senses at the outset, and slay this sinful destroyer of *gnana* and *vignana*!"

It is difficult to get rid of all desires. All we can do is try to minimise our wants and needs. As individuals, we may not find it easy to battle our own inner urges; but under the guidance of a realised soul who is desire-less, who is positive, who is kind and compassionate, we may find the mental strength to conquer desire. Who better than Sri Krishna to show us the way? To conquer desire, and to find the perfect remedy against all sorrow and suffering, call upon Sri Krishna. Once Sri Krishna enters your life, those predatory desires—*trishna* will lose its hold on you and let go of you. And you will progress towards a life of peace and harmony.

How may we conquer lust?

1. Sri Krishna's words give us the best way to accomplish this: "Therefore, knowing that the consciousness is superior to the intelligence, steady your mind by self-realisation and conquer this insatiable enemy, Lust." (Gita—III-23)

    As the Lord tells us in the Gita, cultivating the higher awareness or God-consciousness is the first step. Therefore, let us rise, rather than fall in love with God! Make God your father, your mother, your friend, your beloved! Let everything you do strengthen this relationship which is the embodiment of the highest love we are capable of!

2. Realise that he who loves God fears to do anything which displeases God. Therefore, live a life of purity.

3. Know that pure love is unselfish and thrives on sacrifice; therefore, go out of your way to love all creation, and help as many as you can.

4. If your friends and your surroundings are leading you to thoughts of lust, change your environment! This includes avoiding books, internet content and other material which rouses your lower passions.

5. Practise meditation; introspect on the goal of your life and find your vocation, your calling.

6. All impure actions and impulses begin with thoughts. Therefore, be aware of your thoughts.

7. Never ever forget that you are God's child, and that His help and healing grace are always available to you. Therefore, pray to God and enlist His strength and wisdom to fight your greatest enemy.

Ravana, the many-headed demon in the Ramayana, is the prime symbol of lust. Knowing that Sita is divine and the chaste wife of Rama, he lusts after her and carries her away to his kingdom. Note that he is so powerful that he is virtually indestructible! Certainly there is no living human, no jivatma who can conquer him. Even the devas and the lesser spirits dwell in fear of him; they cannot defeat him or even prevent his evil deeds! Mighty demons like Indrajeet, Kumbhakarna and other rakshasas are ready to die for him!

It is significant that Ravana does not fall easily even to the Divine weapons of Sri Rama. When Rama destroys his chariot, Ravana flies high into the sky and attacks from above. He takes multiple forms to mislead the vanara sena. The arrows and missiles of Laxmana, Hanuman, Angad and Sugreeva, make no impact on Ravana.

It is as if Sri Rama wanted to teach us how difficult it is to overcome lust! Every time he cuts off one of Ravana's heads, another one grows in its place. And Ravana is never stable, never in one place. He is here, there, everywhere. He is not to be underestimated, not to be taken lightly. He demoralises Rama's army. He has several tricks up his sleeve . . .

There is a Ravana within each one of us, the demon of lust and evil desires. Our reason, logic and wisdom tell us that what we are doing is not right; and yet we cannot stop doing it. We are well aware that the consequences of our impulsive, ill-thought actions are going to be destructive and disastrous; but we are impelled by dark forces that we cannot resist.

It is only Rama's arrow—the power of the Name Divine that can destroy Ravana, the personification of lust and illicit desire. Sri Krishna emphasises the same truth: "Surrender unto Me," He tells us, "and I will conquer all your sorrow, sin and suffering!"

Sri Rama will fight our war for us. He will destroy the evil within. He will destroy the Ravana in our hearts. All we have to do is surrender to Him!

PRACTICAL TIP:

If your environment is leading you to thoughts of lust,
change your environment! Start with the small things. Avoid
watching movies, reading books, browsing internet content
or other material that rouses your lower passions. However,
when thoughts of lust overwhelm you, in a masterful stroke
divert your mind to some other inspirational experience
or memory and submerge your mind in the Name Divine.
Repeat the Holy Name until the vicious thoughts leave
you. They are trespassers and should be banished.

Lobha—Greed

Let me begin this section with an incident from our great epic, the Mahabharata: Bhishma Pitamaha, the divine son of the sacred River Ganga, is asked about the source of sin and evil in the world. Bhishma replies to his questioner, Yudhishtira, a young King seeking wisdom. "From greed, sin and all *adharma* flows, a stream of misery. Greed is the poisoned spring of all cunning and hypocrisy in the world. It is greed which makes people sin . . . Greed is the source of evil."

Lobha is a synonym for *ragha*—it means desire, craving, attachment or greed. And when we use the term greed in English, it is generally associated with the craving for more and more money, material wealth, physical comforts and earthly goods. Also called avarice or covetousness, it is a widely prevalent tendency of our consumerist society today.

Like lust, greed is also a severe internal affliction, a diseased condition of the mind that leaves us permanently dissatisfied, permanently insecure and permanently in a state of lack, want and need. As the wise old saying goes, "He who loves money excessively, never has money enough." The more you acquire, the more you covet, and the more you dwell in want and insecurity. An offshoot of this insecurity is the fearful need to hoard, store and cling to the wealth you have amassed.

Greed manifests itself in two broad tendencies—the impulse to hoard and the impulse to spend extravagantly. In the first case, the 'victim' is obsessed with amassing more and more wealth and putting it away safely for a future need. Such a man cannot trust Providence for the morrow: he is determined that he will be his own provider, and will not look to God to take care of his needs; he trusts his avarice and miserliness more than he trusts God's generosity and compassion!

The 'big spenders' as they are called are on an acquisition spree; they cannot stop buying things that they don't really need. Bigger, better, newer, faster . . . whatever the excuse, they keep spending on luxuries and whims, indulging their urge to splurge and acquire more and more . . .

I would say that the tendency to accumulate material wealth, the craving for more and more, is the root cause of human unhappiness. Greed, one of the seven deadly sins, binds people with fetters that shackle their capacity for self-fulfillment and inner harmony. As bestselling author, Dr. Wayne Dyer tells us, "It is just not possible to live one's life in joy and peace within the restricting structures of materialism, greed and accumulation . . . The perpetual pursuit of more and more," he tells us, "only begets loneliness and unhappiness."

The more we are attached to a house, a car, a piece of jewellery or an object, the more we lay ourselves open and vulnerable to unhappiness. The desire to possess leads gradually on to the impulse to accumulate and hoard. Invariably, we begin "keeping up with the Joneses" as they put it in England—i.e. constantly comparing ourselves with our neighbours, and trying to be one up on them.

Our senses are instruments of cognition that God has blessed us with; they tell us to eat when we are hungry and seek warmth when we are cold. The fulfillment of such needs is essential for human survival. It is only when our needs and wants become unreasonable and obsessive that they cease to be natural and enter the danger zone of covetousness.

Artha or wealth, as we saw, is also one of the purusharthas or legitimate goals of life. But we must understand that amassing wealth is not the sole aim of our life on earth: it is only the means to a higher end. Our money, our assets, our car, our house and all our worldly goods (acquired by fair, honest means) can help us and our loved ones lead a life free from want and deprivation. At a higher level, they can help us, help others who are not as fortunate as we are. In other words, wealth is an aid to living life well; it cannot be the be-all and end-all of our life!

Sad to say, our society today recognises and equates accomplishment and success with money. In business, sports or entertainment, a 'star' or a 'leader' is valued by the millions he has amassed, the size of his bungalow and the car he drives. I do not grudge these celebrities the money they make; but I am pained by the fact that we lesser mortals compare ourselves to them, and feel frustrated, inadequate and insecure!

Happiness and success cannot be measured in terms of money, power, position, wealth or social status. For a man may have all of these and still be miserable. The world thinks that a millionaire is a 'successful' man. Success must be measured by the yardstick of inner happiness—your ability to be happy and make others happy; the ability to love and be loved by others; the ability to live in harmony with those around you, with your own self and God's cosmic laws . . .

> Money can buy the husk of things, but not the kernel. It brings you food, but not appetite, medicine but not health, acquaintances but not friends, servants but not faithfulness, days of pleasure—but not peace or happiness.
>
> —Henrik Ibsen

Wealth is equated with power today: display of jewellery, flaunting huge cars and bungalows, throwing lavish parties and influencing others' decisions are all symbols of wealth as well as power; and we know that our most eminent politicians and industrialists are keen to grab as much power as they can, when they have amassed more wealth than they need.

Though greed is concerned with material acquisition, it affects the spirit, for our priorities are mixed up and in the famous words of the Bible, we begin to worship Mammon, rather than God.

Greed is detrimental to human virtues: a greedy person will never give generously; he only wants to take, grab and hoard. Greedy people are obsessed with spending more and more on themselves. Greedy merchants hoard and sell at higher prices to the detriment of their buyers. Worst of all, greedy people sacrifice values like honesty, justice, integrity and fair play in the mad urge to make more money. This is how need and desire turn into avarice and covetousness.

Atheists and agnostics in the west argue that the church has failed to condemn greed as a deadly sin, as it is reluctant to antagonise its own rich and influential members. They point out that religious leaders simply overlook the great inequalities in society and the vast gulf between the haves and the have-nots, justifying the material affluence of those who have too much, while warning the poor that they must not be greedy!

The trouble with many of us is that we try to legitimise greed and avarice as a justifiable, even praiseworthy ambition to become rich and powerful. Personal greed is equated with drive, motivation and incentive to live life well. There is nothing wrong with being wealthy; there is nothing wrong in wielding power; but we fail to realise that greed is not just acquisition of wealth; the problem arises when we do it to the detriment of others, and when we are so engrossed by our selfishness that we deny the claims of our humanity and become self-seeking, manipulative and exploitative. Truly, the avarice for wealth makes people blind to all else.

What is wrong with earning money? What is wrong in accumulating wealth for the security of our loved ones, you might ask. Nothing, if we are able to be content with what we possess. But unfortunately, we do not stop there. We look at others, we compare ourselves with them, and we are unsatisfied if we have less. We are haunted by the greed for more, more and more!

> Covetousness . . . is like an illness . . . It is characterised by an insatiable thirst for riches even though one is already filled with them . . . The illness of insatiability cannot be healed by trying to satisfy the avaricious person's appetite. On the contrary, he must practise simplicity and scarcity. Allowing him to indulge his desire will only exacerbate his illness. Therefore, he who wishes to disentangle himself from greed should practice living modestly.
>
> —Schimmel

When we look at TV commercials and advertisements, every product seems to promise us happiness, fulfillment and complete satisfaction. Thus we fall into the trap of desiring more, acquiring more, possessing more—and more! We are in bondage to our possessions. And they demand more out of us. The bungalow needs to be painted and repaired, it needs security guards; the car needs to be serviced and maintained; the gadgets demand their upkeep. And we carry all these self-imposed burdens for the sake of possessions. But are they truly contributing to our inner happiness?

That is a question which each of one of us has to answer for ourselves.

Let me add, it is not only the great corporate executives and the multi-millionaires of this world who are guilty of greed: the common man is also on the list of the discontented and covetous.

There are several things in our lives about which we are not happy. Our 'wish list' for something different, something more, something other than what we possess extends to several aspects of our daily life.

Many affluent teenagers now carry cell phones—something unheard of even ten years ago. But not all of them are happy with these gadgets. Every six months or so, they wish to change models; they want more 'features'; they want the latest. When they are denied what they want, they sulk, they grumble, they wish they had richer and kinder parents. I am afraid many parents are simply pushing their children into the trap of acquisitiveness and covetousness by their indulgence and 'generous' gifts! Many children from affluent families simply do not know the value of money. As for hard work, it is what others are meant to do to get them what they crave; they are brought up to believe that the world and everything in it is theirs for the asking.

Homemakers, mothers and wives wish to have better equipped kitchens; they want more gadgets, more equipment, more aids to make their life easy. They want better furniture, more expensive curtains, and nicer clothes to wear. Men want a better job, a better boss, a bigger car, more money and more leisure. Why, many graduating students from management and engineering institutes consider it demeaning if they are not offered a six figure salary to start with!

There's nothing wrong in wishing for any of these things. The problem arises when we develop a feeling of active discontent with what we are and what we have. Discontent leads to depression, and depression destroys our peace of mind.

We would do well to recall the words of Jesus: "It is easier for a camel to pass through the eye of a needle than for a rich man to enter the Kingdom of God."

Jesus is not telling us to live in penury; He is only asking us not to be obsessed with material acquisitions and possessions. Greed is not wealth per se; greed is only inordinate, excessive, obsessive need for wealth!

Some of us stoop very low to gain power, position and authority. After all, why are graft, corruption and bribery so rampant in the world today? Why are flattery, falsehood and hypocrisy so prevalent among the mighty and the powerful? Such practices only point to the lowest elements in human nature. They taint our minds and hearts and impede our spiritual progress—the only progress that matters.

> If at all anything must be desired, let it be the desire for freedom from rebirth: this can be attained only by those who desire to be free of all desire.
>
> There is no sorrow for those who have overcome desire; where desire exists, sorrows will come incessantly.
>
> —**Thirukkural**

Let us but ask ourselves: what is it that we seek through wealth, power and sense-indulgence? Where will they lead us eventually? Of what avail is earthly greatness and worldly wealth when we know that the call can come any time for us—and we shall be reduced to an urn full of dust and ashes!

Alas, our minds are scattered. They are dispersed, tainted with desires, they look downwards. We need to purify our minds: we need to raise the level of our consciousness. We must learn to look upward, onward. We need to protect ourselves against the three pronged attack of *maya*—the desire for pleasure, wealth and power.

> Lay not up for yourselves treasures upon earth, where moth and rust doth corrupt, and where thieves break through and steal: But lay up for yourselves treasures in heaven, where neither moth nor rust doth corrupt, and where thieves do not break through nor steal: For where your treasure is, there will your heart be also . . . For what does it profit a man if he shall gain the whole world and lose his soul?
>
> —**The Gospel according to St. Matthew**

How may we overcome greed? So let me offer you a few practical suggestions:

1. Greed is selfishness, self-seeking, self-gratification: Therefore, the basic step to conquering greed is to become selfless. Think less of yourself; think of others. Think of what you can do to make others' lives better. Think of how you can do what you can to alleviate the suffering and misery of others

2. Give, give, give! Those that give, live; those who do not give, are worse than dead! Remember that all that you have, all that you are, all your talents, skills, wealth and comforts are given to you in trust—as a loan—to share with others who are not as fortunate as you are. The impulse to care and share is the best antidote to greed. The new beatitude for the material age is: Give and you shall receive!

3. Cultivate the virtue of detachment: Detachment is a virtue dear to Sri Krishna: learn to overcome attachment to money and material possessions. The Gita urges us to live our life, perform our duties in a spirit of detachment. When we do all that we do in a spirit of offering—*Krishna arpanam*—we learn to rise above low desires. We learn not to cling to our possessions; we learn to give away things instead of holding on to them. We learn to practise selfless service and charity.

4. *Santosha* or contentment is another virtue we must cultivate. When we overcome the craving for more money, more power, more material comforts, we become aware that there is nothing wrong in enjoying the pleasures and the delights of this beautiful world that God has created for us. The only thing that is wrong is selfish attachment and craving for more and more! Contentment is not to be equated with complacency and passivism; it is the dynamic realisation that what we are, and what we have are part of God's providence and God's will for us. It is the awareness that we are

with God in all circumstances and situations of life and therefore, lack nothing!

5. We must also grow in the awareness that we cannot find happiness outside of ourselves! A famous poet—a saint of Maharashtra sings:

> O man, you have roamed a great deal
> In the outer world.
> You have gone hither and thither
> You have picked flowers, fruits and pursued innumerable activities.
> But all you have acquired is weariness.
> Now it is time to soar in the endless inner spaces of your being.
> What you are seeking can be found there
> In it's fullness.

Unfortunately, we are engaged in searching the entire world over for happiness. If we search until our last breath, we are not going to find happiness 'out there somewhere'. We cannot wish for it; we cannot buy it; nobody can hand it over to us on a platter. It is a very personal feeling—and it must come from within!

6. Simplify! Simplify! Simplify! In the words of Thoreau, "Don't burden yourself with possessions. Keep your needs and wants simple, and enjoy what you have. Simplify! Don't fritter away your life on non-essentials. Don't enslave yourself for luxuries you can do without."

A Tale from the Panchatantra

Once upon a time there was a greedy heron who lived by the side of a pond. He was crafty and deceitful, and devised a plan to get a continuous supply of fish for himself. So one day, he went to the side of the pond and put on a gloomy face without attempting to catch any fish.

In the pond lived a wise old crab, which often helped the fish in the pond. On seeing the gloomy heron, the crab asked him what the matter was. The heron said, "Alas! I am worried that the pond is going to be soon devoid of any fish, which are in turn my source of food. I overheard a group of fishermen talking about catching all the fish in this pond with their huge nets. But I know of a pond which is a little farther away, where all the fish shall be safe. If the fish are interested, I can carry a few each day to the other pond where they will be safe."

All the fish were horrified to hear the news and eager to make use of the heron in reaching a safer destination. So everyday some of them volunteered to go with the heron. The heron took some fish each day in the beak, and on reaching a large rock nearby, he would eat up all the fish and leave the bones of the fish scattered on the rock. Thus he was able to get a continuous supply of fish at no effort at all.

One day, curiosity got the better of the crab, and it volunteered to go with the fish. When they got closer to the rock, the crab saw the scattered bones and understood the heron's foul play. Enraged, it tightened its claws around the neck of the heron and snapped his head off. The heron died a gruesome death on account of its greed. The crab crept back to the pond and told all the fish about the lies the heron had been telling.

PRACTICAL TIP:

To counteract greed, learn to give. You can start by visualising the joy of giving. Visualise that a close friend gives you a beautiful coat. You love the texture, the colour; the silk lining feels like love wrapped around your skin. People you don't even know stop and compliment you on your coat. You feel so much pride when you put it on and walk down the street.

As you are strolling along feeling warm and happy, you come upon a homeless person who is freezing on the side of the street. He looks sick and extremely weak. You stop, take off your coat, and give it to him. The person smiles at you and thanks you for your generosity. You see his face lighten up and feel a glow in your own heart.

Gluttony

Perhaps no other religion gives such a special status to food, as the Hindu faith does. Food as *anna* or *prasadam*, is an intrinsic part of all worship, ceremonies and festivals in India. The preparation, actual cooking and the distribution and consumption of food is carried out with respect and reverence, as part of the sacred rites of worship on such occasions. Food is cooked in the faith that it is meant to be an offering to the Lord; it is eaten in the belief that it is a benign blessing that purifies the body, mind and soul of the devotee. *Prasad* that is received at the Guru's *satsang*, which may be very simple or somewhat elaborate on special days, is regarded as a gracious gift that brings with it the blessings of the Master.

Hindus worship Annapurna as the Goddess of food and cooking. Annapurna is depicted in Indian iconic art as a lady holding a pot overflowing with grain, empowered with the ability to supply food to an unlimited amount of people. She is thought to be an incarnation of Goddess Parvati, the wife of Lord Shiva. The food she provides is not just physical nourishment, but a divine blessing that gives us the energy (*Shakti*) to achieve knowledge and enlightenment.

As such, Annapurna or Anna Lakshmi also symbolises the divine aspect of nourishing care. Food is cooked with a spirit of sanctity, as an offering to God, and eaten as *Prasad* in many Hindu homes. We find images of Annapurna in several hotels, restaurants and kitchens, as well as in large dining halls where hundreds of people sit down to eat a community meal.

Under these circumstances, we might be forgiven for wondering how and why the consumption of food became associated with a negative trait: the answer is again in the degree of desire: when this becomes excessive or inordinate with respect to food, we become slaves of gluttony or *atyahara*, as it is called in Sanskrit.

The truth is that food is not just nutrition and sustenance to the pious Hindu. The dictum, *You are what you eat,* has a special significance in our scriptures and our ancient wisdom. When it comes to the practise of *abhyasa* or self-discipline, what we eat, how we eat and how much we eat are equally important. This is why gluttony, or excessive indulgence in food becomes a *vikshepa*—or obstacle on the path of spiritual life; in this as in other indulgences of the flesh, excessive attention to the cravings of the senses, (in this case, the sense of taste) is seen as detrimental to one's higher needs, i.e. food for the spirit.

Gluttony is over-indulgence in or over-consumption of food and drink. Its root lies in the very expressive Latin term *gluttire*, which means to gulp or to swallow hastily. Gluttony is associated not only with over-indulgence and excessive consumption but also with extravagance, wastefulness and indifference to the needs and wants of others. This is why very many people in India frown on extravagant banquets and lavish parties in a poor country like ours, where millions are forced to go with barely one meagre meal every day. If nature dictates that we must eat to live, gluttons are those who live to eat.

A practitioner of Yoga whom I had met recently described the contemporary attitude to food as "perverse and dysfunctional". We do not regard food as a necessity for sustenance; in fact, necessity or hunger or even nutrition is no longer the concern of many people: they eat to satisfy their craving, their appetite, rather than eat for their energy or work requirements. Often, such people put into their mouths things which are meant to 'tickle their palate' or satisfy their craving—the kind of 'junk food' condemned by health-conscious people. What is even more frightening is that overeating has now become routine with many people. We eat more than we need; we eat too frequently; we eat food that is not good for us; we eat the wrong combination of foods; we eat too much of what we like. Spicy, oily, high-calorie foods, fattening sweets and desserts, excessive intake of alcohol and the presence in our food of harmful additives, colours and preservatives and on top of it all, erratic meal-times—the whole thing adds up to the excess of gluttony!

> Mind is manufactured out of the food that we take. The subtlest part of food reaches upward to the heart and thence entering the arteries . . . and thereby bringing into existence the aggregate of organs of speech and being changed into the form of the mind, it increases the mind.
>
> —Swami Sivananda

Overeating is not just an excess, a sin and a negative trait: it is a serious disorder that can lead to various medical problems such as obesity, hypertension, coronary diseases, depression, stroke and arthritis. In other words, gluttony is as much a disease of the body as it is a sin of the spirit!

> Gluttony denotes, not just any desire of eating and drinking, but an inordinate desire . . . leaving the order of reason, wherein the good of moral virtue consists.
>
> —St. Thomas Aquinas

Sadly, most of us indulge in overeating without realising the implications: all we are aware of is the momentary pleasure of the eating experience. We are "wedded to the pleasure of the table" as the euphemism goes; or we have made a god of our belly, as St. Paul put it!

One of the worst forms of excessive gluttony is depicted in history books that depict the fall of the 'great' Roman empire: I refer to what is called sbinge-eating in modern terminology. As we know, people can eat only so much: more food beyond this point will only make us sick. Some people in the Roman banquets refused to recognise this limitation of the human digestive system. They were so addicted to their food and drink that they would stuff themselves at these banquets, go out and force themselves to throw out or vomit all that they had eaten and return to the banquet for more! It was against this kind of excess that early converts to Christianity took to the habit of fasting, as 'mortification of the flesh' and the curbing of appetite.

St. Thomas Aquinas tells us that we fall a prey to gluttony in the following ways:

- Laute—eating food that is too luxurious, exotic or costly
- Nimis—eating food that is excessive in quantity
- Studiose—eating food that is too daintily or elaborately prepared

- Praepropere—eating too soon, or at an inappropriate time
- Ardenter—eating too eagerly.

He also observes that the first three ways are related to the nature of the food itself, while the last two have to do with the time or manner in which it is consumed.

Nutritionists tell us that we can never overeat if we stick to the right kinds of foods; this is because our intake is then conditioned by hunger and monitored by our brain and we know exactly when to stop. Have you ever heard of anyone stuffing themselves with carrots or salads or sprouted *moong*? On the other hand, it is the wrong kinds of food that make us overeat: with reference to ice cream, chocolates, fried food and junk food, we exclaim: "I can't stop eating!" We look at enormous empty plates and we say, "I can't believe I ate all that!" In this case, we are being controlled by appetite, and the brain's sensors cannot control our urge. This is why overeating is regarded as a psychological or emotional disorder.

> The food that we eat is transformed in three different ways; the gross or the heaviest part of it becomes the excrement; that of medium density is transformed into flesh and the finest part goes to form the mind.
>
> —Chandogya Upanishad

We eat for several reasons: hunger is the foremost; but there are other reasons like satisfying the cravings of our appetite (which is usually for the wrong kinds of food); on social occasions like parties and banquets; for celebrations and 'treats' given by our friends; and sometimes to escape from a bad mood or even to avoid boredom. There is also the phenomenon of emotional eating, when we consume excessive quantities of the wrong kinds of food in response to feelings other than hunger. Depression, boredom, stress and anger also trigger off excess eating. (There are people who, when travelling by train, will get off at each station to eat something, and also eat in between.) Experts tell us that obesity has now assumed epidemic proportions in the world of the affluent.

A recent survey conducted in the US revealed that between the ages of 20 and 50, the average person spends about 20,000 hours—over 800 days—eating. People's daily schedules, according to the survey, are often planned around mealtimes. Business deals are cut among people who "do" lunch together. At home, families have TV dinners; on the way back from shopping or work, mothers take children along to fast-food drive-up windows, and most cities have a thriving ordering service on the phone.

We need to rediscover the advantages of fasting, which is as integral to the Hindu way of life as *prasad*, which we spoke of earlier.

Fasting means abstaining from all food and leaving the stomach empty for a few hours or a few days. This is not to be confused with starving—for fasting is undertaken intentionally, with the aim of cleansing or detoxifying the system. By abstaining from all food and restricting our system to the intake of water or liquids alone, we enable our system to cleanse itself. During a fast, this is what happens to the system:

- All the toxic wastes accumulated in the body are thrown out—in the form of phlegm, faeces or gas.
- The reserves—in some cases, the excess—of carbohydrates, fats and vitamins that have been built up in our system, are used up efficiently and effectively.
- The body becomes light, agile and alert.
- No harmful side-effects are produced.

People today are so addicted to eating that they even snack between two main meals. Even when they work, they take a 'coffee break' or 'tea break'. When they go to the movies, they take popcorn or chocolate or ice cream with them. When they have nothing to do, they eat just to pass the time. When they watch TV, they like to munch on something: Thus constant eating has become part of our social behaviour. Some people even get up from sleep for a midnight snack!

How can the human digestive system function efficiently when it is constantly misused in this way? It is little wonder that digestive disorders are common among the affluent nowadays.

Our ancestors knew the remedy for it: habitual fasting on certain days of the week or month. Thus, people in India still observe a fast on holy days like *Ekadashi, Chaturthi* or on certain days of the week like Mondays or Saturdays.

Fasting is an excellent process of self-discipline. It is one of the safest and quickest ways to rid the body of toxins. Fasting is also one of the best ways to clear the brain, enabling it to operate at peak efficiency. The Red Indians of America believed that fasting gave rise to wisdom.

Most religions of the world recommend fasting to the devout. Christians fast during Lent. Jews fast on the eve of all their feasts. Muslims fast during Ramzan.

Mahatma Gandhi fasted several times during his life—often up to twenty days or more. He fasted not only for health—but also for moral and political considerations. Even after India's independence, he fasted to reconcile Hindus and Muslims in Calcutta.

How can you overcome gluttony and its associated eating disorders? So let me offer you a few practical suggestions:

1.   Identify those triggers that cause you to overindulge in food: they may be social, emotional, psychological or simply contextual or situational. Therefore, dieticians recommend that we keep a food diary to note exactly what we eat and when, as also what thoughts or moods trigger off pangs for food. Once you become aware of your eating patterns, try and find an alternative to food in such situations. For example, if you are bored and have nothing much to do, you might go for a walk

or read a book instead of choosing a snack. If you are busy and overworked, you might try having fruits or nuts instead of junk food.

2. Start the day with a good breakfast. Do not skip meals as this might lead to unhealthy snacking or extra large portions at the next meal.

3. Portion control is very necessary! Learn to eat less of everything rather than denying yourself anything. Some Oriental cultures serve food in smaller sized plates so that people serve themselves less food, rather than overloading their plates.

4. Plan your meals properly so that you don't end up eating "whatever is available" which is usually the wrong kind of food, or order junk food on the phone.

5. Many people agree that eating out, as it is called, or eating at restaurants and clubs often leads to excessive intake of food and drink. Large portions are served in such places; there are several courses to each meal; and the food and desserts are tasty and offer us the kind of variety that we cannot get at home. The result is that many people end up making gluttons of themselves and live to rue it with indigestion, acidity and other ailments. As far as possible, avoid eating out, if you cannot discipline yourself; if it is unavoidable, order less and share each portion with friends. The other day I read that several upper crust restaurants in the West are now thinking of imposing a special tax of 20% on the bills of dinners who actually order too much food and waste it!

6. Remember the precept of Lukman, who was a physician and healer of antiquity. One day a man came to him and requested him, "Tell me in a few words, the secret of good health." Lukman's reply was indeed significant: "*Kam Khao, Gham Khao,*" he said to the man!

Kam Khao means eat less. We must learn to eat less than we think we need. Quite often we eat when we are not hungry. Many people (quite unnecessarily) eat four meals a day. Still others are misled by false hunger—which is probably nothing more than sheer boredom, or lack of anything meaningful to do; so they resort to eating, only to feel forthwith, a sense of heaviness or flatulence. We must learn to eat in moderation. Some people think they need to eat till their stomachs are full. But in reality, our stomach must be only half-filled with food; the other half should be air and water. If we fill our stomach with fast food, junk food or an excess of carbohydrates and fats, we are bound to suffer from the ills of overeating.

7. Watch what you eat! Flesh foods, foods of violence may build up your fat—but they will not give you a radiant body, which is vibrant and vital. Animal food is unacceptable on three counts—humanitarian, aesthetic and hygienic. The trouble with modern day eating is that it is excessively made up of food of violence!

8. Salads, fruits and fresh vegetables are rich in vitamins. They build up health and vitality. Fasting once a fortnight flushes out the impurities in the system, renews and refreshes us physically and mentally. It speeds up the flow of currents of life-force within us. When fasting is accompanied by silence or *maun*, the mind becomes clearer and stronger. Inner and outer are in perfect tune.

9. Drink plenty of water! Water helps to flush out the toxic wastes in our body. It controls the body temperature by being given out as perspiration. Experts have calculated that there is a daily loss of four and a half pints of water through our skin, lungs, kidneys and alimentary canal. Needless to say, this loss must be replenished. It is good to drink water whenever you are thirsty. However it is better to drink water after a meal than with it.

10. As far as possible, stick to a *satvic* diet. [See box for more details]

The Gita tells us that food is of three types—*satvic, rajasic* and *tamasic.*

Satvic foods contribute to inner calm and peace of mind. They induce pious thoughts and feelings. They keep us in a state of emotional poise and equanimity.

Rajasic foods incite passion and give rise to restlessness.

Tamasic foods induce dullness, inertia and lethargy.

They also give rise to impure thoughts.

Satvic food gives us just the right amount of energy—not too much or too little. But *satvic* food is easily digestible, leaving us with sufficient energy balance to devote to our work. It is rich in proteins, carbohydrates, vitamins and fibres. *Satvic* food also calms our senses.

Rajasic foods give us plenty of energy—but we spend much of it in digesting and eliminating such food. As it contains energy-enhancers, there is greater likelihood of toxin build-up in the body, if this energy is not fully utilised. Ayurvedic physicians tell us that rich foods in this category generate stress, causing respiratory, renal or cardiac disorders. *Rajasic* food also causes obesity, diabetes and ulcers.

Tamasic food gives very little energy—but is difficult to digest. It also generates a lot of toxins in the system.

The ideal diet is one that avoids *rajasic* and *tamasic* foods. You will not be surprised to know that what the ancient Hindu scriptures regarded as *satvic* food is now held up to be the ideal food—although by other names! Experts call it high—fibre, natural, anti-oxidant, etc. and we are encouraged to eat more of such foods. As for what the sages called *rajasic, tamasic* food—the very same foods are now labelled high-fat, high—cholestrol, carcinogenic, etc. and we are warned to keep them out of our diets to the greatest extent possible!

Satvic food is preferred by men of purity. It promotes integrity, intelligence, intellectual brilliance, strength, vigour, health, pleasure of physical and mental life, cheerfulness, delight and the true joy of living. As Sri Krishna tells us in the Gita;

The foods which prolong life and promote purity, strength, health, joy and cheerfulness, which are sweet, soft, nourishing and agreeable, are liked by *satvic* men.

XVII—8

Satvic foods are palatable, savoury, sweet, juicy and health-giving. They are agreeable to the taste, too. These are foods such as wheat, rice, green beans, dairy products, fruits, vegetables, etc.

We must eat *satvic* food, for it purifies heart, mind and body. Remember too, *satvic* food is the product of honest work! If you eat food purchased with ill-gotten money, or received as a gift from a person who is not honest, you are not eating *satvic* food! Remember the story of the holy man, who after great persuasion, consented to accept *biksha* at the house of a known evil-doer: when he left the man's house, he found to his horror, that he had actually stolen some silver articles that belonged to his host—the food that he had accepted at the hands of the evil-doer, had actually turned the holy man into a thief!

Man is what he eats—according to a German proverb. The mind is also a product of the food you eat. So, you must be careful! Eat food that is cooked by a person whose vibrations are pure. The right persons to feed you are your mother, wife, daughter, sister and your Guru.

Before you begin to eat, mentally offer your food as an *ahuti* to the Lord: then your food will give you strength for work and service. Also, when you are eating, make sure that the atmosphere around you is peaceful. Do not eat in a noisy environment.

Satvic food not merely appeals to the tongue, it is a source of nutrition to mind and body. Naturally, vegetarian foods such as fruits, milk, nuts, lentils and vegetables are the best kind of *satvic* food.

Tamasic food is stale, rotten and impure. This includes all foods of violence as well as food left overnight. In the modern context one should also include the intake of alcohol, hallucinogenic drugs as well as smoking as *tamasic*. The *tamasic* person derives pleasure from such habits.

Rajasic food is the food of passionate men—men who are energetic, worldly minded. These foods are bitter, sour, salted, over-hot, pungent, dry and biting—eg. opium, tobacco, tamarind, chillies, parched grain, rye, etc. Such food produce pain, grief and sickness.

In general, *rajasic* foods are over-cooked, over-spiced, laced with artificial colours and preservatives. Such foods lose their vitality. Excessive use of salt, sugar, onion, garlic and other spices also makes food *rajasic*. Such food may please the palate—but it cannot keep the body healthy. They produce excessive toxins, leading to various ailments. Such foods are also not conducive to the practice of meditation, reflection or spiritual enquiry.

PRACTICAL TIP:

Gluttony and overeating never ever give you extra energy or satisfaction. Lethargy or *tamas* is a state induced by overeating, or over indulgence. You begin to feel low and depleted, 'heavy' in body and mind; you find that you cannot do anything useful or constructive. Our moods have a definite bearing on our minds, and it is better that we avoid such conditions.

Simple exercise to avoid overeating: Learn to eat mindfully! Develop eating competency skills!

9

Envy and Jealousy

I cannot help thinking that envy is one of the most demeaning emotions that human beings can ever give in to!

Lust, greed, gluttony, fear and anger are all corroding, poisonous and self-destructive: but the reason I call envy the worst of them all is that it makes us unhappy on account of another's happiness, success or good fortune. In other words, we are constantly watching others and the way they are leading their lives and burn with jealousy and bad feeling when good things happen to them. We resent others' success; we negate their success and their accomplishments; we want what we do not have; we do not want others to have what they have. What a way to live! How degrading for a human being to give in to such meanness and spite!

Envy is closely allied to multiple negative traits: covetousness or *matsarya* (craving to possess what is not ours): jealousy or *asuya* (excessive fear of losing what we have, extreme attachment and possessiveness); resentment and bitterness at the good that happens to others.

Envy leads to ill-will, destructive thinking, constant criticism of others, disliking others for their good qualities, denying and negating their talents, skills and achievements, and rejoicing in the misfortune or downfall of others.

> Too many Christians envy the sinners their pleasure and the saints their joy because they don't have either one.
>
> —Martin Luther

Dante defined envy as, "a desire to deprive other men of theirs." In fact, he groups envy with anger and pride as the sins of "Perverted Love". Anger is "Insufficient Love" and pride is "Excessive Love of Earthly Goods". Envy is perverted because it "loves" what other people possess, rather than aspiring to what is Good, Beautiful and True. In its rejection of what is good, in its craving for the material over the spiritual, envy is seen as "eating away" the heart of the envious person. Dante shows the envious as among those farthest away from Paradise, with their eyes sewn shut, but weeping over their sins. Again, a common metaphor for Envy is "wearing out the eyes". Envy goes directly against the Ten Commandments, specifically, "Neither shall you desire . . . anything that belongs to your neighbour." In Dante's Purgatory, as we saw, the punishment for the envious is to have their eyes sewn shut with wire because they have gained sinful pleasure from seeing others brought low. Thomas Aquinas described envy as "sorrow for another's good". An old Tamil proverb pictures the condition of the envious graphically, "When others prosper, they starve themselves."

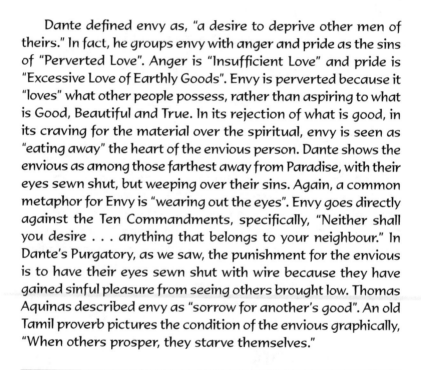

> A man that hath no virtue in himself, ever envieth virtue in others. For men's minds, will either feed upon their own good, or upon others' evil; and who wanteth the one, will prey upon the other; and whoso is out of hope, to attain to another's virtue, will seek to come at even hand, by depressing another's fortune.
>
> —Francis Bacon, Essays, "Of Envy"

In our great epic, the *Mahabharata*, Duryodhana is the very personification of envy: he is envious of Bhima's prowess; he is envious of Arjuna's skill as an archer; he is envious of Yudhishtira's goodness; he is envious of the Pandavas' prosperity and popularity among the people. Burning in this fire of envy, he turns to his father, King Dritarashtra, "Father! The prosperity of the Pandavas (my younger brothers) is burning me deeply! I cannot eat, sleep or live in the knowledge that they are better off than I am!" His envy drives him to every vicious act that is possible: gambling, cheating, falsehood, attempted murder . . .

Another character that readily springs to mind as an archetypal symbol of envy is Satan, in Milton's *Paradise Lost*. Satan as we might say, takes the cake: he envies God's glory and power; in his blind covetousness, he imagines that he can actually take God's place as the King of the angels and Heaven; he becomes the creator and the original inhabitant of hell and hell-fire, which is the fire of all-consuming, all-negating envy!

> There was a preacher who was offended because he was not invited to join a friend's picnic. But the invitation came to him well before the appointed day. All he could say was, "It's too late; I have already prayed that it should rain."

Someone whom I met once argued with me that it is old-fashioned and superstitious to put down envy as a sin: he put his point forward forcefully, "Dada, envy is legitimate when it urges us to fight injustice; envy is legitimate when it propels us to aspire to greater heights and achievements through ambition. Why should I rejoice in another's good fortune? Why should I not resent inequality among people? Injustice is even more sinful than envy; and ambition is as much a virtue as love or charity!"

I told him that Bertrand Russell, a noted agnostic, had also expressed a similar opinion; Russell actually felt that envy was the driving force in the movement towards democracy, as manifested in historical events such as the drawing up of the Magna Carta in England and the great French Revolution. But in the final analysis, Russell warned that envy could only lead to human unhappiness.

It is a false proposition that makes envy out to be a great leveller of inequality and injustice. The trouble is, it levels down, it does not level up! If everyone can't be rich, it argues, let us make the rich poorer! If we cannot have what others have, let us take away what is theirs! If someone is happier than we are, let us make him miserable like us!

I must add for the benefit of my friend and others like him: there is a basic confusion of terminology and attitudes here. Legitimate ambition, the desire to prove oneself, the desire to achieve the best that one is capable of, can manifest itself in success without resenting others; and the desire to fight injustice, the desire to right wrongs and eliminate inequality, can be inspired by motives higher than mere envy. In fact, psychologists have even begun to talk of two kinds of envy: malicious and benign. The former is and will remain a corrosive negative emotion: the latter can be the impetus, the motivation to achievement and social justice. Like righteous indignation which stands up to fight wrongdoing, the benign impetus to do the best for oneself and others is wholly free of the negativities of jealousy and ill-will.

> While it is true that envy is the chief motive force leading to justice as between different classes, different nations and different sexes, it is at the same time true that the kind of justice to be expected as a result of envy is likely to be the worst possible kind, namely that which consists rather in diminishing the pleasures of the fortunate than in increasing those of the unfortunate. Pssions which work havoc in private life work havoc in public life also. It is not to be supposed that out of something as evil as envy good results will flow. Those, therefore, who from idealistic reasons desire profound changes in our social system, and a great increase of social justice, must hope that other forces than envy will be instrumental in bringing the changes about.
>
> —**Bertrand Russell, Conquest of Happiness**

The ancient Greeks tell us this story of a man who was granted a boon by Zeus: there was a single condition attached to the boon; whatever the man got, his neighbour would get twice as much. He asked for a chariot; he got one, and the neighbour got two. He asked for a mansion, the neighbour got two of the same. In desperation, he asked to lose one eye, so that his neighbour would lose both eyes!

> Reflect on this: God has made us what we are and placed us where we are. Envy is a sign that we think He made a mistake. The wise prophet asks us: "Since you object to what God does, can you expect Him to do what you want?"

Envy is often used interchangeably with jealousy: there is a difference between the two in terms of the degree of feeling and the target of the feeling: to put it simply, envy is directed towards objects and material possessions. Thus, I feel a pang of resentment and malice when I see the brand new car my neighbour has bought, and compare it unfavourably with the small, old car that I drive. Jealousy is concerned with people, relationships and attitudes. Thus I feel sidelined and ignored, when my colleague is praised by the boss, or my wife praises a friend of mine for his qualities, attributes or achievements. At heart, jealousy is fear of losing something which I possess—the love of my wife, the respect of my colleagues or the admiration of my boss. It is said that envy involves two people, while jealousy involves three; but I think this is an oversimplification! There are people like Duryodhana who are envious of everything and everyone in the opposite camp; there are people too, like Othello, who is tortured by a purely sexual jealousy of his young, innocent wife. ". . . the green eyed monster that doth mock the meat it feeds on . . ."

This is how Shakespeare describes jealousy in his tragedy *Othello*, which is a classic illustration of this ruinous passion. Jealousy indeed is like a virulent cancer that consumes us from the inside. There are men too, like Iago in the same play, who are jealous of others' good name, reputation and virtue!

The subtle semantic differences between envy and jealousy are not our concern: suffice it to say that we must try to overcome these negative traits in all their aspects howsoever they may manifest themselves in our individual lives. And we would do well too, to remember that the highest and the best among us can fall a prey to these traits: King Kaushika was at first envious of the cow that was tethered to the humble *ashram* of Sage Vashishta; then he grew jealous of the Sage's power of *tapasya*; when he finally attained the sought after status of *Brahmarishi*, he needed Vashishta's approval for the same! But we must not forget that he obtained perfect grace only when he recognised his weakness and conquered the unworthy emotion of jealousy and sought the grace of the Sage whom he had envied in the first place!

I must add too, that envy can sometime manifest itself in the petty but despicable trait of constantly criticising, finding fault with others and belittling their achievements.

There are several triggers to envy: the wealth, fame, beauty, material possessions, good reputation, power, popularity, success or happiness of others. For this reason, envy is thought to be closely linked to the eye—the evil eye, if we may call it that, which cannot bear to see another's good fortune. But if we are to understand envy for what it is, we may 'see' that it is a sin of perception rather than sight: to our jaundiced view, the happiness of others is intolerable and we "turn green with envy", as the saying goes.

> Every other sin hath some pleasure annexed to it, or will admit of an excuse; envy alone wants both. Other sins last but for awhile; the gut may be satisfied, anger remits, hatred hath an end, but envy never ceaseth.
>
> —Robert Burton, The Anatomy of Melancholy

Such envy does not just consume us: it may lead to even more grievous wrongdoing such as hatred, violence, aggression and the desire to destroy what we crave but cannot have. Many of us shudder to think of the evil queen in the fairy tale who was determined to kill Snow White just because the girl was younger and more beautiful than her!

Envy takes many forms.

Envy of possessions says, "I wish I had your house or car or clothes."

Envy of position says, "I wish I had your job or honorary degrees."

Envy of privilege says, "I wish I had your freedom or opportunities."

Envy of people says, "I wish I had your good looks or education or talent."

—Anonymous

Sad to say, envy is its own punishment! Bitterness, frustration, resentment and self-hatred are some of its worst afflictions which rebound on the envious heart! What causes envy?

1. The desire for more, greed and covetousness.
2. Issues with our own self-image; low self-esteem.
3. Focussing on lack and deprivation rather than blessings and advantages.
4. Unhealthy comparisons with others.
5. Acute consciousness of self-limitations and inferiority (sometimes imaginary).
6. Unhealthy attitude and mistrust in close relationships.
7. Pessimism, melancholy, depression—all leading to a warped attitude and skewed perspective on life.
8. Sheer malice—the refusal to "live and let live".

As I said, envy is its own worst punishment; the envious soul dwells forever in misery, frustration and unhappiness. The consequences of envy are devastating, for it can consume us, destroy us from within.

1. We are unable to focus on our life, our needs and our aspirations; we are constantly looking at others and judging them.
2. We rush to condemn, criticise and evaluate others, even when it is none of our business.
3. We become spiteful and wish ill of others.
4. We destroy friendship, healthy competition and worthwhile relationships.
5. We give in to slander, malice, gossip and vicious attacks on others.
6. We bring misery into the lives of our near and dear ones as well as ourselves, by refusing to be happy, contented and peaceful.

How may we overcome the poisonous, cancerous traits of envy and jealousy? So let me offer you a few practical suggestions:

1. We must realise that envy can do us far more harm than it can do to those whom we envy. Envy leaves us miserable and frustrated and bitter: the person against whom it is directed, may not even be aware of our meanness towards him; and if our envy shows up so openly that he is aware of it, it can only lower his opinion of us!
2. In spiritual terms, envy is an offense against God, for it leaves us ungrateful to God for His many gifts, while we pine for all that we do not have. The antidote to this is to thank God all the time, for the countless blessings he Has conferred upon us. Where gratitude to God is, there can be no envy of our fellow human beings.
3. An effective and constructive way to overcome envy is to send out love and blessings to our rivals, when an envious thought so much as crosses our mind. Thus, if you are envious of X, utter a silent prayer: "May God bless dear X! May he/she always be my friend!"

4. Try and appreciate your rivals for their genuine achievements. Admiration and appreciation are positive, energising emotions, and will draw what you admire into you!

5. As they say, imitation is the best form of admiration! By imitation I do not mean blind copying, but rather emulating or becoming like the people whom we admire. Emulate the winning traits of your rivals—like punctuality, courtesy, pleasant manners, honesty, efficiency, time management, etc. Not only will this enhance your performance but also add to your self-esteem and make you feel proud of yourself.

6. Envy is negative: aspiration is positive. Therefore, visualise yourself succeeding, achieving your goals like those whom you admire. But don't just stop with daydreams; turn your dreams and aspirations to reality by taking concrete action to achieve what you desire.

7. An idle mind is always likely to fall a prey to negative traits like envy. Therefore, let us engage ourselves in constructive good work—like selfless service and offering help to people who need it. When we focus on constructive tasks, negativities are driven out.

8. Nurture a healthy sense of self-esteem by becoming aware and appreciative of your own good qualities. Remember that you are unique, and that God created you for a special purpose.

9. Avoid comparing yourself, your status, your possessions and your achievements with others. Unfavourable comparisons only lead to frustration. Realise that each one of us has our own role to play in the eternal drama of life.

10. Anything that causes the mind to lose its balance is detrimental to our happiness; and the best way to restore the mind to balance and harmony is to practise the virtue of contentment. Prayer and recitation of

the name Divine are quick and easy ways to attain contentment.

11. Let us learn to be moderate in our desires. It was a wise man who prayed, "Give me neither poverty nor riches! Give me just enough to satisfy my needs! For if I grow rich, I may become content without God. And if I am too poor, I may steal and covet what is not mine."

12. Robinson Crusoe, alone on his desert island, says, "I do not possess anything I do not want, and I do not want anything I do not possess." Contentment can come from wanting less and feeling more grateful for what we have.

For him who constantly meditates upon My presence within all persons, the bad tendencies of rivalry, envy and abusiveness, along with false ego, are very quickly destroyed.

—**Srimad Bhagavatam 11.29.15**

ஒ௰ ௫௭

PRACTICAL TIP:

The first and the last step to overcome jealousy is to learn
to accept yourself, love yourself and develop awareness
of your weaknesses and insecurities. Rid your mind
of old thought patterns and negative thinking habits.
Erase negative thoughts that lead you to jealousy and
replace them with thoughts of gratitude—for what you
are, what you have and what you can achieve if you try!
Use your energy to create the person you want to be!

௫௭ ஒ௰

10

The Secret of an Integrated Personality

What is an integrated personality? To give you a textbook definition, it is a personality type combining or coordinating separate elements so as to provide a harmonious, interrelated whole.

A well-integrated personality is also a well balanced one, in which emotions, feelings and thoughts are in equilibrium. An imbalanced personality is one in which the person is often overcome by the excess of certain feelings or emotions like greed, passion, anger or depression.

A friend once asked me, "In this age of stress and tension, when people are being buffeted by recession, unemployment, uncertainty and fragile relationships, is it really possible for us to become well-balanced, well-integrated personalities?"

I replied to him, "Now, more than ever, it is important for people to strike that balance within! For we may not be able to control all that happens outside of us, but surely, our emotions and feelings must remain within our control!"

> So divinely is the world organized that every one of us, in our place and time, is in balance with everything else.
>
> —Johann Wolfgang von Goethe

Let me repeat, a well-balanced personality must be the first and most vital step to happiness in life. And true happiness, as I have emphasised from the start, is your *birthright*. Yes, *ananda*, bliss, the peace that passeth, nay, surpasseth understanding is your birthright! You are a child of God—and He is the source of eternal bliss, unending bliss. The moment you realise that you are a child of God, you will not let externals affect you negatively. The realisation that you are God's child, a spark of the Supreme Self, will allow you to transcend all sense of frustration and limitation that you might feel as a limited, powerless human being trapped in a situation that he cannot control. All you need to do is forget your lower self—and realise your true self as a child of God. When we forget this outer self, transcend the phenomenal, material world, we draw closer to the real, inner self, which is peace.

In Chapter Two of the Bhagavad Gita, the Lord gives us a wonderful picture of the *stitha prajna*, the balanced man:

> A man with a disciplined mind, who moves among sense objects, with the senses under control and free from attachment and aversion, he rises to a state of *prasadam*, peace . . . Having attained peace, there is for him an end of all sorrow; of such a man of peace the understanding soon attaineth equilibrium.
>
> —Chapter II, 64, 65

These *slokas* emphasise the great truth that only a person who is *not* disturbed by the incessant flow of desires can achieve peace; not the man who strives to satisfy desires. These *slokas*,

I am told, were very dear to the heart of Mahatma Gandhi. He had them recited everyday at his prayer meetings.

This is the first step to attaining peace of mind, and a balanced personality: that is, to attain the realisation that all that happens, happens according to the will of God.

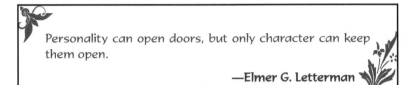

Personality can open doors, but only character can keep them open.

—Elmer G. Letterman

Why is it that we lose our balance? Because our wishes, our desires, are thwarted. We want a particular thing to be done in a particular manner. We expect an action to have a certain outcome. We expect people to react or respond to us in a particular way. When it happens in a different way, perhaps in exactly the opposite way, we lose our balance.

Why do we feel upset, frustrated, disappointed? Because we are attached, because we are involved. If I do my work, if I live my life with detachment, as if I am playing a part, I would not be upset.

Gurudev Sadhu Vaswani used to tell us, "God upsets our plans to set up His own. And His plans are always perfect."

If I have the faith that whatever has happened to me is according to the plan of the Highest, that there is some hidden good in it for me, I will not be upset! Gurudev Sadhu Vaswani also used to say, "Every disappointment is His appointment. And He knows best."

Once you realise this, there is no more frustration, no more unhappiness. You abide in a state of tranquility and peace. You may not be able to achieve this straight away. It is a process through which you must move.

As my friend rightly pointed out, we live in an excited, agitated world—a world beset with stress and strain. This intensified stress and strain manifests itself physically as heart disease, hypertension and nervous breakdown. Doctors agree that the cause of such ailments is psychological rather than physical.

> You were intended not only to work, but to rest, laugh, play, and have proper leisure and enjoyment. To develop an all-around personality you must have interest outside of your regular vocation that will serve to balance your responsibilities.
>
> —Grenville Kleiser

The great athletic trainer William Muldoon once said, "People do not die of disease, they die of internal combustion."

Our ancestors in India were fond of saying: "*Man durust, tan durust.*" If the mind is at peace, the body is bound to be hale and hearty.

It all sounds so simple and logical; when we cultivate the spirit of acceptance, we acquire inner peace; our minds are balanced, our bodies healthy and our hearts are happy.

May I offer you five simple steps to achieve balance and inner harmony?

1. Begin the day with God:

"Can you have your concert first and tune your instrument afterwards?" a spiritual teacher asks us. The answer is obviously, "No we cannot". "Therefore," he continues, "begin your day with God."

The first thing we do on getting up in the morning shapes the entire day. Does it not stand to reason that we should begin the day right?

Many people I'm afraid, spoil their mornings by waking up with a feeling of restlessness, irritability and tension. How sad this is!

Every morning, when you wake up, there is a choice before you: you can choose optimism, faith, positive thinking and right attitude; or you can choose pessimism, defeat, negative thinking and despair. What would you choose?

Begin the day well—and God will take care of the rest of the day!

Everyday, as you wake up in the morning, let there be a prayer on your lips, a simple prayer. Let me share with you the prayer that I offer to God:

> O Lord! This new day comes to me as a gift from Thy spotless hands. You have taken care of me throughout the night, and I am sure You will keep watch over me throughout the day. Praise be to Thee, O Lord. Blessed be Thy Name. Blessed be Thy Name. Blessed be Thy Name!

You can reword this prayer if you like, in your own way. But make sure you begin the day by remembering God—with a prayer on your lips.

When you begin the day with God, you will find yourself remembering Him throughout the day. In the midst of your work, you can pause, and out of the depths of a love-filled heart, say to God: "I need You God! I cannot do without You!"

So I urge you once again. Begin the day with God. And hold fast to Him throughout the day. He will fill your day with the happiness and peace that passeth, surpasseth understanding.

2. Let your mind rest in God:

The second step to interior peace centers around the words of the great Jewish Prophet Isaiah:

Thou wilt keep him at peace whose mind is stayed on Thee.

The Prophet was speaking out of experience. He had discovered the secret of true and lasting peace. He must have found that every time his mind stayed on the Lord, every time he felt he was in the presence of the Lord, he was at peace.

Thou wilt keep him in perfect peace whose mind is stayed on Thee!

Our minds are restless. They are restless like storm-tossed boats. Our minds wander here and there. Our feet may be firmly planted on the earth—in Pune, New York, London or Singapore. But our minds wander to the four corners of the globe!

How many months, how many years it takes for a rocket to reach a distant planet like Saturn? But if you think of that planet, it is there in your mind—you are there in thought. Your thought moves faster than sound or light. Your mind will not be confined by any limits or barriers. The mind is its own space; the mind is its own power. This is certainly a good thing for the mind.

But the negative aspect of this is that the mind is restless. It cannot be still; its feet are burning; it cannot stop; it will not stay in one place; it keeps on wandering!

Thou wilt keep him in perfect peace whose mind is stayed on Thee!

Can you try a little exercise? Every time you become aware that the mind wanders, quietly, gently, lovingly, sweetly, bring the mind back to the Divine Presence. It is not easy! Even as you become aware that the mind is wandering, you are wandering with the mind! However, do your best to stop the wandering mind in its tracks, and bring it lovingly back to the Divine Presence.

> The most important human endeavour is the striving for morality in our actions. Our inner balance and even our very existence depends on it. Only morality in our actions can give beauty and dignity to life.
>
> —Albert Einstein

Do not attempt to fight the mind—for the mind can be a formidable enemy! Make friends with it. Say to it gently, as you would tell a stubborn child, that it would be good for it to focus on the Divine Presence. Allow your mind to savour the peace that this can bring. Say to it, "See, see how happy we are sitting in His Divine Presence! He will keep us in perfect peace when we rest in Him. Why can't we sit at His Lotus feet, and experience the bliss of life?"

Repeat this simple exercise over a period of three to six months. You will be amazed at the change that this brings about in your life! Your life will become new!

When your mind wanders, and you become aware of it, bring it back to the Divine Presence. *Thou wilt keep him in perfect peace whose mind is stayed on Thee!*

Recently, a survey conducted among young students in urban India revealed that many of them spent on an average, between 2 to 3 hours *per day* on their cell phones. They said they were not talking all the time; they spent much of their time sending messages.

I once saw someone sending several 'SMSs', or text messages as they are called. I think we cannot have a more apt demonstration of the restless, wandering mind than the act of frantically pressing buttons on a small instrument. Trying to communicate through one's fingertips. I am told that a little boy in the UK damaged his right thumb beyond repair through constant messaging!

It is not just that our mind keeps wandering during the day, it is not at rest even when we fall asleep. I watch people sleeping—and I find their brows knit with frowns. The calm, relaxed look which you find on a baby's face when he is asleep, cannot be found on the face of a sleeping adult. This is because we are worrying, worrying all the time. We cannot switch off our anxiety and worry, even when we are asleep.

Ashantasya Kutah Sukham! The disturbed mind is far from peace. How can it mediate? How can it be at peace? How can it even be happy unless it is established in God?

So it is that Gautama the Buddha tells us in forth right terms: There is nothing so disobedient as an undisciplined mind; and there is nothing so obedient as a disciplined mind.

Let your mind be the master of your body: therefore, let the mind be disciplined and obedient. As the great Greek dramatist Euripides puts it, "The wavering mind is but a base possession."

The wandering mind makes mountains out of molehills and perceives insurmountable obstacles on the path of progress. On the other hand, the focused mind acquires the wisdom, strength and power to help us face the challenges of life.

In the words of the Zen Philosopher, Chang Tzu: "If water derives lucidity from stillness, how much more the faculties of the mind! The mind in repose, becomes the mirror of the universe, the speculum of all creation."

Thou wilt keep him in perfect peace whose mind is stayed on Thee!

3. Count your blessings:

A few years ago, when I was in the US I gave a talk on, "How to make problems work for you." On the very next day, a brother wrote to me, "I am on a gloomy express train carrying an excess of negative baggage. What can I do to get off this grouchy track?"

Then and there I put down a few words on paper—I wrote a small poem which I would like to pass on to you. There is not much of music or imagery in it, but I do believe that if we all follow the teaching it has to offer, it will be to our advantage:

> When all is dark as a starless night
> And there's not a ray of hope in sight
> Then count your blessings one by one
> You will be amazed at all that God has done!

When we are feeling slightly ill, just a little feverish, we rush to the medicine cabinet. At the slightest hint of a headache, we go in search of Advil or Paracetamol. At the least hint of acidity, we keep Pepcid or Digene handy. But when the mind is upset, when the mind is sick with worry, anxiety and negative thinking, we do nothing! We just wallow in our misery, we allow ourselves to suffer "on the gloomy express", with our "excess negative baggage", as my friend put it so picturesquely!

Let me offer you a prescription for an 'upset mind'. It is a prescription you can write out for yourself! Just take a sheet of paper and write on it all the things for which you are grateful to God.

When I offer this suggestion to my friends, many of them respond, "What have I got to be thankful for? Nothing!"

> When you stand with your two feet on the ground, you will always keep your balance.
>
> —Tao Te Ching

Do you know the value of your eyes? Do you know the value of your ears? Your hands? Your feet? Your mind? Your family and friends? If someone were to offer you a million dollars, would you give away your eyes? Should we not feel grateful to God for the gifts He has bestowed on us—two eyes with which to see the beauty of the world around us, two ears with which to hear music, song, conversation and children's laughter; two hands with which to do a thousand things; two feet which can take us wherever we choose to walk!

And that is not all. He has given us people who love us— family, brothers and sisters, friends and well-wishers!

> Count your blessings instead of your crosses
> Count your gains instead of your losses
> Count your joys instead of your woes
> Count your friends instead of your foes
> Count your smiles instead of your tears
> Count your courage instead of your fears
> Count your full years instead of your lean
> Count your kind deeds instead of your mean
> Count your health instead of your wealth
> Love the world as much as you love yourself
> Count your blessings!

When you become aware of 'abundance' in your own life, your attitude to circumstances will change and you will be ready to take on 'lean' and 'dark' days with a more positive and constructive attitude. This sense of 'abundance' will add to your faith and contribute to your inner balance and harmony.

4. Accept the Will of God!

May I pass on to you a *mantra* which is sure to bring you peace? It is a prayer which a saint, a holy man of God used to offer again and again. Inscribe it on the tablet of your heart. Repeat it again and again—remember it by day and night, for it is really simple:

Yes Father, Yes Father—Yes and always yes!
Yes Father, Yes Father—Yes and always yes!

There are people who are upset with me because I advocate the philosophy of acceptance. They say to me, that this will make people lazy and lethargic; they will give up all their drive and ambition and simply sink into passive resignation.

I beg to differ! People who believe in the supremacy of the Almighty, people who learn to accept His Divine Will, never ever give in to lethargy and pessimism. They do as the Lord bids them in the Gita—they put in their best efforts; they do not slacken; they do their best to achieve what they want. But if they do not achieve the desired results, they do not give in to despair and frustration; they do not give in to disappointment.

Acceptance in the spirit of gratitude unlocks the fullness in our lives. It can turn despair into faith, strife into harmony, chaos into order, and confusion into clear understanding. It restores peace into our hearts and helps us to look forward to the morrow in the faith that God is always with us!

It is not enough to speak of gratitude or enact deeds of gratitude—we must *live* gratitude by practising acceptance of God's will in all conditions, in all incidents and accidents of life.

When things are not going as we wish, we tend to develop 'tunnel vision'—that is, focus on the dark, negative side of life. However, we will do well to remember that it is always darkest before dawn and trial and adversity can be powerful agents of change that help us grow, evolve to become better human beings, and eventually make a success of our lives.

There are several things in our lives about which we are not happy. Our 'wish list' for something different, something more, something other than what we possess extends to several aspects of our daily life.

When the 'wish list' becomes an obsession, we start blaming God for all the ills that beset us!

- God could have made me taller, slimmer, more beautiful.
- God could have given me more money, a richer husband, a more understanding wife, kinder parents, better friends.
- God could have made my children more intelligent, more accomplished, more obedient, more appreciative . . .

The list is endless!

So the blame shifts to God! Are we not accusing Him of being unfair, unjust and unkind when we perceive our life to be all wrong? In the end it all turns out to be His fault!

Patience and acceptance are difficult to cultivate. Without them, there can be no inner development, no spiritual growth.

That is not at all! When we lack the wisdom to accept God's will, we cause ourselves a lot of unnecessary grief; grief that arises because reality differs from our wishes and our plans.

Wisdom consists in accepting God's will—not with despair or resignation, but in peace and faith, knowing that our journey through life has been perfectly planned by Infinite love and Infinite wisdom. There can be no mistake in God's plan for us!

To seek refuge is to trust the Lord—fully, completely, entirely. It is to know that He is the one Light that we need in the darkest hours of our life. He is the all-loving One whose ears are ever attentive to the prayers of His wayward children. He is the all-knowing One who does the very best for us. With Him, all things are possible: and if He chooses *not* to do certain things for us which we want Him to do, it is not because He cannot do them, but because He knows better—He knows we require something else for our own good.

So it is that he who has taken refuge in the Lord is ever at peace. "Not my will, but Thy will be done, O Lord," he prays. Whatever happens, "I accept! I accept! I accept!" is his *mantra*. "Yes Father, yes and always yes!" is his response to all incidents and all accidents of life. Nothing—no accident, no loss, no tragedy—can disturb his equanimity.

5. Pray without ceasing:

If you would have inner peace, pray without ceasing! This is one spiritual discipline that can go on forever! You cannot sit in meditation very long. You cannot fast longer than a few days. Every other spiritual discipline has its limitations as far as the average man is concerned—but prayer can go on forever!

You will find the following injunction in the Bible:

> Be anxious for nothing, but in everything, by prayer and supplication with thanksgiving, let your requests be made known to God. And the peace of God, which surpasses all comprehension, shall guard your hearts and minds . . .

We are actually ordered—indeed commanded—not to worry, not to be anxious, but to pray specially for our requests; pray with thanksgiving. And we are promised that when we do so faithfully, God's peace will guard our hearts. What a wonderful promise this is!

Prayer is a very simple matter. For me, it is just speaking with God. He is with you everywhere: He is available to you at all times. You will never find His line 'busy' or 'engaged'. Reaching Him on the prayer-line is quicker than the 'speed dial' on your cell phone. All you have to do is think of Him, shut out the world momentarily, and start a loving conversation with Him. If you wish, it can go on and on and on!

We waste much of our time in activities of no account. Our mind is so distracted, it keeps running from pillar to post. Why not engage this distracted mind in a loving, intimate conversation with God?

Prayer need not be a complicated affair. Suppose a friend drops in for a visit. Wouldn't it be natural for you to welcome him, discuss your plans, dreams and aspirations with him? Would you not seek his help and support in all that you do? This is exactly what you must do in your prayers, too—for God is the Friend of all Friends.

You must remember too, that what is impossible with man is possible with God. Whenever you find yourself in a difficult situation, passing through a period of darkness, there is One who is always there with you. A loved one may be afflicted with an incurable illness—and the doctors give up hope. You are on the verge of bankruptcy—and there is no one you can ask for help. You are in a personal relationship crisis—and the bond seems near breaking point. You have done your very best, but you are unable to solve the problem.

Just hand it over to God!

How can you hand it over to God? Go to Him in prayer. In prayer, place the problem before Him. Tell Him, "Lord, I can do nothing in this matter without You. It is for You to come and help me out."

But remember to *thank* the Lord before you close your prayer. Pray with thanksgiving. Thank the Lord as though He has already answered your prayer. Only remember that His answer may take a while to reach you. Feel that you are well and happy. Feel that your problem has been solved. Allow gratitude to well up in your heart, and you will find that peace fills your mind simultaneously.

What is impossible with man is possible with God! Keep on shooting prayers! People tell me, "Dada, it's alright for you to tell us to pray ceaselessly—but we simply do not have the time!" I say to you, *make* time for prayer. Even as the needle of the compass always points towards the north, our hearts and minds should always turn towards the Lord!

Praying ceaselessly is not a ritual; it is not about words or gestures. It has been described as a constant state of awareness of our oneness with God. You may of course, ask for all the good things you need—and you may gain the faith that it is all obtainable to you. For all prayer is effective—but ceaseless prayer has multiplied effect.

It was Jesus who said to us, "The Kingdom of God is *within* you." Ceaseless prayer will help you discover that Kingdom and enter within. You identify yourself with your own divinity. Not only do you find inner harmony and balance—but you also become empowered to pass it on to others around you. You spread harmony, you radiate peace, you share the gift of joy with everyone who comes into contact with you.

I have spoken to you of five simple steps to inner balance. These are not the only means, nor are they exhaustive or arbitrary. My intention has been to examine closely, certain important aspects of inner balance. Once we become aware of these aspects, we can take one step at a time, choosing whatever is easiest and appeals most to us. I would like to tell you something very important: once we have taken the first few steps, we will walk all the way to balance, peace and harmony, all the way without ever turning back—for the journey is as peace-filled as the destination!

PRACTICAL TIP:

Resolve today that you will cast away all negativities even as we cast away our old garments—negative attitudes, bad habits of frustration, resentment, anger, envy and jealousy. Resolve to put on new and fresh garments—garments of light that cast no shadow, garments of radiance that would make us worthy participants in the festival of life that God holds for us every day!

Tell yourself: I want to become New! I want to drop my old habits, negative ways of thought, and become quite, quite new! Imagine, you are inhaling the fresh air that God is sending out to you for each and every breath you take. Each and every breath is new and fresh! Each second, each moment of this life is fresh and new! Breathe in the fresh air! Inhale deeply, with each new breath you take. Feel yourself becoming new and fresh with every breath you take! Tell your self: I want to become new! I want to become New! Visualise yourself, radiant, happy, contented, deep within! See yourself smiling, happy, at peace with yourself